TOO
MANY
<u>TIMES</u>

TOO MANY TIMES

HOW TO END GUN VIOLENCE IN A DIVIDED AMERICA

 MELVILLE HOUSE
BROOKLYN · LONDON

TOO MANY TIMES

First published in 2020 by Melville House Publishing
Copyright © Melville House Publishing, 2020

First Melville House Printing: October 2020

Melville House Publishing
46 John Street Brooklyn, NY 11201

and

Melville House UK
Suite 2000 16/18 Woodford Road London E7 0HA

mhpbooks.com
@melvillehouse

ISBN: 978-1-61219-879-8
ISBN: 978-1-61219-880-4 (eBook)

Library of Congress Cataloging-in-Publication Data 2020942670

Designed by Beste M. Doğan

Printed in the United States of America
10 9 8 7 6 5 4 3 2 1

A catalog record for this book is available from the Library of Congress

CONTENTS

PART I

HOW WE LIVE NOW

96 Minutes

BY PAMELA COLLOFF

On the morning of August 1, 1966, not long before summer classes at the University of Texas at Austin were about to let out for lunch, an architectural engineering major named Charles Whitman arrived at the Tower dressed as a maintenance man. He would be described the following day in the Austin American as "a good son, a top Boy Scout, an excellent Marine, an honor student, a hard worker, a loving husband, a fine scout master, a handsome man, a wonderful friend to all who knew him—and an expert sniper." The footlocker he wheeled behind him contained three rifles, two pistols, and a sawed-off shotgun, as well as a cache of supplies (among them canned peaches, deodorant, an alarm clock, binoculars, toilet paper, a machete, and sweet rolls) that suggested he planned to stay awhile. After a receptionist switched on an elevator that Whitman had been trying in vain to operate, he smiled and said, "Thank you, ma'am. You don't know how happy that makes me."

Whitman rode the elevator to the twenty-seventh floor, dragged his footlocker up the stairs to the observation deck, and introduced the nation to the idea of mass murder in a public space. Before 9/11, before Columbine, before the Oklahoma City bombing, before "going postal" was a turn of phrase, the 25-year-old ushered in the notion that any group of people, anywhere—even walking around a university campus on a summer day—could be killed at random by a stranger. The crime scene spanned the length of five city blocks, from Twentieth to Twenty-fifth streets, bounded by Guadalupe ("the Drag") to the west and Speedway to the east, and covered the nerve center of what was then a relatively small, quiet college town. Hundreds of students, professors, tourists, and store clerks witnessed the 96-minute killing spree as they crouched behind trees, hid under desks, took cover in stairwells, or, if they had been hit, played dead.

Both the Associated Press and United Press International would rank the shootings as the second most important story of the year, behind only the war in Vietnam. But until 1999, when the university dedicated a memorial garden near the Tower to the victims, the only physical reminder on campus of what had taken place were the few remaining bullet holes left in its limestone walls. (Many of the original scars had, over the years, been filled in with plaster.) No plaques had ever been displayed, no list of names read, no memorial services held. Decades of institutional silence had turned the shootings, and Whitman himself, into the answers to trivia questions. But, of course, there was nothing at all trivial about that day.

To mark the fortieth anniversary of that day, we asked the people who were there to tell their stories.

"THERE'S A SNIPER UP ON THE TOWER AND HE'S SHOOTING PEOPLE!"

Whitman's first shot was fired at 11:48 a.m.

SHELTON WILLIAMS *was a senior at UT. He is the director of the Osgood Center for International Studies, in Washington, D.C.* It was a few minutes to noon, and I was driving down the Drag in my brand-new red 1966 Mustang. My sister-in-law was visiting from Midland, and I was kind of showing off Austin to her. It was a bright, sunshiny day. I remember "Monday, Monday," by the Mamas and the Papas, playing on the radio. We got to the stoplight that's right there outside of the University Co-op Bookstore, and that's when I heard it. A lot of people thought it was a car backfiring or a sound they just couldn't discern. I attribute this to the fact that I'm from West Texas, but I knew immediately that it was gunshots.

JOHN PIPKIN *was a senior. He is a retired money manager in Houston.* A couple of buddies and I had gone down to Scholz Garten to get lunch before we had to go to work that afternoon. We were eating sandwiches when some guy busts open the door and jumps up on the bar and starts screaming for everybody's attention. He's yelling, "You gotta hear what I'm saying! There's a sniper up on the Tower and he's shooting people!" Everybody in the place starts laughing and saying, "Yeah, right—a sniper on the Tower. Let's drink to the sniper!" So everybody raises their beers and makes a big joke out of it. The guy says, "No, I'm serious. There's a sniper up on the Tower and he's shooting people!" And about that time, we started to hear sirens.

BRENDA BELL *was a junior. She is an assistant features editor at the* Austin American-Statesman. The anti-war movement wasn't very big yet on campus when this happened. The guys still had short haircuts and the girls had flips. We were right at the end of that era, with the Peter Pan collars and the circle pins and the Pappagallo shoes and the fraternity and sorority parties. Random violence and mass murder wasn't something we knew. If this happened now, there would almost be a feeling of having seen it before. But we had no reference point then. We weren't even scared at first. We were just wildly curious. I was in Shakespeare class when it started, and we all ran to the windows of the English building, which is now Parlin Hall, and stood there peering out over each other's shoulders.

CLAIRE JAMES *was a freshman. She teaches elementary and junior high school in Tucson, Arizona.* My boyfriend, Tom Eckman, and I were drinking coffee at the Chuck Wagon when we decided that we'd better put another nickel in the parking meter. We were walking across the South Mall, holding hands, when all of a sudden I felt like I'd stepped on a live wire, like I'd been electrocuted. I was eight months pregnant at the time. Tom said, "Baby—" and reached out for me. And then he was hit.

MICHAEL HALL *was a history professor. Now retired, he lives in Austin.* There was a loud crack outside Garrison Hall that sounded like a rifle shot. I went outside to see what was going on, and I saw a body lying there on the cement in the middle of the mall, in the very bright sunlight. To my left, there were three live oak trees, magnificent specimens with very large trunks. A young man was crouched down behind one of them, his fingertips touching the bark, terrified, staring up at the Tower.

DAVID BAYLESS JR. *was a freshman. He sells insurance in Denison.* I ran toward Batts Hall, and I'd just gotten inside when the bell rang. People started pouring out of classrooms; it was lunchtime and everyone was in a hurry. I held my arms out and tried to block the doors that led out onto the South Mall. I didn't scream or holler. I just said, "Don't go out there. Someone's shooting people." But no one believed me. They looked at me like I was a dumb kid and pushed right past.

CLAIRE JAMES: Tom never said another word. I was lying next to him on the pavement, and I called out to him, but I knew he was dead. The shock was so great that I didn't feel pain; it felt more like something really heavy was pressing down on me. A conservative-looking guy in a suit walked by, and I yelled at him, "Please, get a doctor! Please!" even though I still didn't understand what was happening. He looked annoyed and said, "Get up! What do you think you're doing?" I think he thought it was guerrilla theater, because we had started doing things like that to bring attention to the war in Vietnam.

BOB HIGLEY *was a junior. He is the managing director of an investment firm in Houston.* To me, the university had always seemed like an idyllic place that was separate from the rest of the world. It was devoted to ideas and learning. You could say whatever you wanted to say; you could be provocative if you wanted to. The campus was smaller then, and the student body was nearly half the size it is now, so there was a real sense of community. It was shocking to me that one person, a fellow student, could ruin all that so quickly. He was killing indiscriminately, aiming wherever he saw targets—riding their bicycles, looking out windows, walking down the Drag.

GAYLE ROSS *was a junior. She is records supervisor at the Plano Police Department.* I knew this was no ordinary day. It had that same feeling of time isolated, of before and after, that the Kennedy assassination had. My reaction was "Oh, no, not again." You knew that after this day, this moment, nothing would ever be quite the same again. There was a quality of suspended animation. Normal life had stopped, and for this little space of time, everything revolved around the Tower and that man.

"... HE SEEMED LIKE A NICE, CLEAN-CUT, ALL-AMERICAN KIND OF GUY."

By three o'clock on the morning of the shootings, Whitman had stabbed and strangled his mother, Margaret, in her apartment and stabbed his wife, Kathy, in their bed as she slept. In the half-typed, half-handwritten letter he left on Kathy's body, he wrote, "Lately (I can't recall when it started) I have been a victim of many unusual and irrational thoughts . . . I talked with a doctor once for about two hours and tried to convey to him my fears that I felt come overwhelming violent impulses [sic]. After one session I never saw the doctor again, and since then I have been fighting my mental turmoil alone, and seemingly to no avail. After my death I wish that an autopsy would be performed on me to see if there is any visible physical disorder . . . Maybe research can prevent further tragedies of this type."

DAVE MCNEELY *was a reporter in the Houston Chronicle's Capitol bureau. He is a syndicated newspaper columnist in Austin.* I met Charles Whitman that summer at his birthday party. I was there by virtue of the fact that the lead guitar player in my rock band was a close friend of his. Whitman was blond, good-looking, solidly built. I remember he seemed like a nice, clean-cut, all-American kind of guy. I was really sort of stunned when I heard the news.

BARTON RILEY *was an instructor in architectural engineering. A retired architect, he lives in Kerrville.* Charlie was one of my students. He didn't have many friends, but he and I had both been in the Marine Corps, and we got along pretty good. From what I understood, his father was a rather crude man and had kicked him around a bit. Charlie felt tremendous anger toward him. When he came to the university, he wanted to excel; he wanted to show his father up. He felt that he had to make A's, and if he didn't, he was very hard on himself.

SHELTON WILLIAMS: I had a class that spring in the architecture building, and I was always compulsively early. So was another guy, Charlie, whose last name I didn't know until I saw his picture in the paper. He always chewed on his fingernails while he read over his notes. I'd never seen anyone work so vigorously on their fingernails; I couldn't believe there was anything left to chew. I remember a kid walked up to him once and said, "Say, Charlie, are you going to go to Vietnam and kill Charlie?" The kid thought that was hilarious. Whitman said, "The Marines can kiss my red-white-and-blue ass."

BARTON RILEY: Charlie called me at eleven o'clock one night and said, "I need to see you." I said, "Now?" and he said yes. So I turned the porch light on and waited for him. He was one of those guys who got red-faced when he was upset, and he was very flushed when he walked in the door. He was carrying an architectural drawing that I suppose he wanted to show me, but the moment he saw that I had a baby grand in my living room, he dropped his papers, sat down, and played "Claire de Lune." It's a fairly tough little tune to play, but he did it beautifully. Then he played something else, though I don't remember what. When all that red had drained out of his face, he stood up. I said, "Well, I'll see you in class tomorrow, Charlie." He said, "Okay," and left.

GARY LAVERGNE *is the author of* A Sniper in the Tower: The Charles Whitman Murders. Whitman had been thinking about doing this for a while. In early September of 1961 he was standing on the seventh-floor balcony of the Goodall Wooten dorm, looking at the Tower, when he turned to a friend and said, "You know, that would be a great place to go up with a rifle and shoot people. You could hold off an army for as long as you wanted." He wasn't like you or me; instead of seeing the Tower, he saw a fortress. Instead of rain spouts, he saw gun turrets. It never occurred to his friend that he might be serious.

"WE WALKED OUT ONTO THE OBSERVATION DECK AND ENJOYED THE VIEW . . ."

The day before the shootings, a teenager from Rockdale named Cheryl Botts (now Cheryl Dickerson) came to Austin to visit her grandmother. When she arrived at the Greyhound station, she met UT student Don Walden, and they struck up a conversation. Walden offered to show her around campus the next day on his motorcycle, and she accepted. They arrived at the Tower the following morning, not long before Whitman took control of the observation deck. The Gabours, a family visiting from Texarkana, arrived soon after.

CHERYL DICKERSON *was a freshman at Howard Payne University, in Brownwood. She is a textbook consultant in Luling.* We walked out onto the observation deck and enjoyed the view on all four sides, looking down at the whole city. I grew up in a very small town, so the thing that impressed me was how big everything was. I mean, there were buildings and highways for as far as you could see; it just went on and on, and it was so beautiful. We looked around for at least a half an hour. We didn't know much about each other, so we did a lot of visiting too.

DAVID MATTSON *was a Peace Corps trainee living in Austin. A retired teacher, he lives in Hastings, Minnesota.* I'm reminded of the article that was in *Time* magazine a week or two later that compared the shootings to Thornton Wilder's novel *The Bridge of San Luis Rey*. In the book, people from all walks of life were, for various reasons, drawn together by fate to a critical time and place in space. Everyone was there for a different reason when the bridge, which spans a gorge in Peru, collapses and they fall to their deaths.

CHERYL DICKERSON: We stepped back inside, and I noticed that the receptionist was not at her desk, but I just assumed she had gone to lunch. The next thing I saw was this reddish-brown swath that we had to step over. My instinct—I mean, I'm a naive small-town girl, okay? I had a rationalization for everything—was that someone was about to varnish the floor. So we stepped over it, and immediately to our right, a blond guy stood up. We had surprised him, apparently. He was bending over the couch, and we found out later that he had put the receptionist's body there and that she was still alive at that time. He turned around to face us, and he had a rifle in each hand. Don thought—I know this sounds crazy—that he was there to shoot pigeons. So I smiled at him and said, "Hello," and he smiled back at me and said, "Hi." All of this took about fifteen seconds; we never stopped walking. We walked to the stairwell and went down one floor to the elevator. I figured out later when I read the newspaper that while we were going down in one elevator, the Gabours must have been coming up in the other.

MICHAEL GABOUR *was a cadet at the U.S. Air Force Academy, in Colorado Springs, Colorado. He owns a radio station in Port Douglas, Australia.* After getting off the elevator, we began the climb to the observation deck. A desk had been pulled across the doorway at the top of the stairs, so I volunteered to go up and inquire whether or not the observation deck was closed. My brother, my aunt, and my mother followed slightly farther behind. As I reached the top of the stairs, I saw a pretty-good-sized blond dude wearing aviator shades running toward me. The barrel of what looked like a sawed-off automatic twelve-gauge shotgun was coming up to firing position. In nanoseconds my brain tried to process the images for a response. I had just started to turn toward my family when the first blast caught my left shoulder. I'm not sure if it was that round, or one of the many subsequent ones, that killed my brother and my aunt.

HERB RITCHIE *was a sophomore. He is a criminal defense lawyer in Houston.* I was in the classics department, on the highest floor of the Tower, just below the observation deck, helping an assistant professor catalog some cards for his dissertation. There was a really loud noise that sounded like filing cabinets had fallen down the stairs. Professor Mench ran to the stairwell and went up the steps a partial distance. He came running back and said, "There are bodies in the stairwell."

MICHAEL GABOUR: I regained consciousness when my father tried to pull me down the blood-filled hallway. I told him to go for help, and he did. I tried to escape but realized that I was unable to move my left leg. I became aware that my mother was still alive, so I kept her that way by not letting her drift away.

HERB RITCHIE: We barricaded ourselves inside an office in the classics department. I put a rolling blackboard up against the door, and we shoved a desk up against that. There were about eight of us, including two nuns. One of the sisters talked about the poor, twisted soul up there who was shooting people, and I thought that was a nice attitude to have, but from where I was sitting, I could see the bodies lying on the mall. I didn't have much sympathy for whoever was up there shooting. I didn't have much sympathy at all.

". . . HE WAS SHOOTING AND KILLING PEOPLE A LONG WAY OFF, ALL UP AND DOWN THE DRAG."

In the first few minutes of Whitman's killing spree, many students were unaware of what was happening; some thought it was the work of drama students or an experiment being performed by the psychology department or just a joke. Claire Wilson (now Claire James) found herself stranded on the South Mall, eight months pregnant and hit in the abdomen. She and other victims lay where they had fallen on the hot cement and tried to play dead. But Whitman never shot again once he had hit his target. In the sniper tradition of "one shot, one kill," he never wasted a bullet on someone who was down.

CLAIRE JAMES: I didn't know it at the time, but I was losing a lot of blood; I felt like I was melting. The heat was just deadly. The pavement was so hot that it was burning the backs of my legs.

DAVID MATTSON: I was walking with two other Peace Corps volunteers, Roland Ehlke and Tom Herman, down the Drag; we were headed to Sheftall's jewelers, because I needed to get my watch fixed. We'd had a water fight at our dorm the night before, and I'd gotten water under the crystal. I was showing my friends my watch—I had stopped and was holding my hand up by my head, at eye level—when all of a sudden my hand came crashing down. The terrific force of it spun me around, and when I looked down, I saw that part of my wrist had been blown away. Ehlke was bleeding too. The manager inside Sheftall's pulled us into the store, and we crawled on our hands and knees behind the display cases.

ANN MAJOR *was a senior. She is a romance novelist living in Corpus Christi.* I went down to the basement of Parlin Hall, and people were panicking. We listened to the radio and realized he was shooting and killing people a long way off, all up and down the Drag. I remember hearing the radio announcer say he had shot a boy off his bicycle near the Night Hawk restaurant, several blocks away.

KAY BAILEY HUTCHISON *was a law student. She is the senior U.S. senator from Texas.* I was in class when the shooting began. We were told that there was a shooter in the Tower, and we watched from the front lawn of the law school. We could see the smoke from the gun each time it fired, although we did not know at the time that he was marking innocent people.

BILL HELMER *was a graduate student in American history. He is a historical-crime writer living in Boerne.* I made my way to the east window in the Texas Union stairwell and was more or less marveling at this nut on the Tower until a shot came in through the open window and hit the arm of the guy beside me. Then I got a wee bit rattled. I thought, "Son of a bitch! This guy is *good*."

JOHN PIPKIN: He was picking people off at incredible distances and hitting them where he could do the most damage. I heard about a guy who was eating a sandwich in the front yard of the Kappa house, minding his own business, when he was shot through the chest.

GARY LAVERGNE: The farthest casualty was well over five hundred yards away, at the A&E Barber Shop, on the Drag. A basketball coach named Billy Snowden saw what was happening on the news and got out of the barber's chair to get a better look. He was standing in the doorway, with his smock still on, when he was shot in the shoulder.

CLAIRE JAMES: A really lovely young woman with red hair ran up to me and said, "Please, let me help you." I told her to get down so she wouldn't attract attention, and she lay down next to me. It was a beautiful, selfless act. I told her my name and my blood type, and she made sure to keep me talking so I wouldn't lose consciousness. She stayed with me for at least an hour, until people came and carried me away.

DAVID MATTSON: We thought that perhaps Sheftall's was being robbed, so Tom Herman and I locked ourselves in the back lavatory. It was sheer terror not knowing if we would be able to escape or if someone was going to come back there and finish us off. A policeman finally pounded on the back door and said, "There's an ambulance just a couple of doors down, so make a run for it." By the time we got to the ambulance, the driver had been shot. He was laid out in the back. We squeezed in beside him, and the policeman took us to the hospital, driving down alleys and using buildings for cover.

ROBERT HEARD *was a reporter for the Associated Press. Now a non-fiction writer, he lives in Austin.* Ernie Stromberger, of the *Dallas Times Herald,* and I drove to campus and parked behind two highway patrol-men who were putting together their shotguns. We figured they were headed for the Tower, so we started following them. When they ran across Twenty-fourth Street, Ernie stayed put; I followed, a few seconds behind them. Just before I reached the curb, I was shot down. I'd forgotten my Marine training; I hadn't zigzagged. It felt like someone had hit my shoulder with a brick. I staggered another three yards and fell in the street.

JOHN ECONOMIDY *was a senior and the editor of the Daily Texan. He is a criminal defense lawyer in San Antonio.* I saw an ambulance round the corner by Hogg Auditorium and stop for two students who had been shot. Both kids had chest wounds and were bleeding through their mouths and noses. I tried to help load them in, and then I took off for the *Texan.* When I ran into the newsroom, I saw a couple of my photographers just standing there, looking through the venetian blinds. I said, "Get off your butts. Get out there and win the Pulitzer Prize!"

ROBERT HEARD: As soon as I hit the pavement, I sat up. I was wearing a white shirt and blood was cascading down it. Some people in the Biological Sciences Building yelled, "Lie down! Lie down!" Either they or another group of students—I never knew who they were—ran out

14

into the street, knowing they could be shot, and dragged me under the trunk of a Studebaker. Ernie Stromberger called in to the *Times Herald* and said, "Tell the people at the AP that they no longer have a man on the job."

HARPER SCOTT CLARK *was a junior. He is the Killeen bureau reporter for the* Temple Daily Telegram. I went to Scholz's at around 12:10 or so, and it was packed. There was a black and white TV running in a corner of the main barroom. Everyone was standing around with their mugs and pitchers because there was nowhere to sit. There was a businessman standing near me—your typical good old boy in cowboy boots and pressed jeans and Western-style shirt—and he said, "Well, I hope they get him off that Tower pretty quick, because the anti-gun people are going to go crazy over this."

"IT SEEMED LIKE EVERY OTHER GUY HAD A RIFLE."

Students waited and waited for the police to arrive. The shootings would spur the creation of SWAT teams across the country, but at that time, the Austin Police Department had no tactical unit to deploy. Its officers had only service revolvers and shotguns, which were useless against a sniper whose perch was hundreds of yards away. Communication with headquarters was difficult, with few handheld radios, and the phone system was jammed across the city. Some officers went home to get their rifles; others directed traffic away from campus. In the absence of any visible police presence, students decided to defend themselves.

JAMES DAMON *was a graduate student in comparative literature. A retired real estate investor, he lives in Austin.* My wife was six months pregnant, and she was stuck on the fourth floor of the Tower, in the stacks. I looked around and didn't see any police, so I went home and got my gun. It was an M1 carbine, which I'd bought for $15 when I was discharged from the Army. I went to the top of the new Academic Center and tried to keep out of sight. That was the closest I could get. I only saw him once, long enough to take aim, but from time to time I would shoot over the ledge of the observation deck and try to hit him.

CLIF DRUMMOND *was a senior and the student body president. He is a high-tech executive in Austin.* Students with deer rifles were leaning up against telephone poles, using the pole, which is rather narrow, as their shield. And they were firing like crazy back at the Tower.

FORREST PREECE *was a junior. A retired advertising executive, he lives in Austin.* I saw two guys in white shirts and slacks running across the lawn of the Pi Phi house, hustling up to its porch with rifles at the ready. Someone was yelling, "Keep down, man. Keep down!"

BRENDA BELL: I don't know where these vigilantes came from, but they took over Parlin Hall and were crashing around, firing guns. There was massive testosterone.

J. M. COETZEE *was a Ph.D. candidate in English literature and linguistics. A novelist who won the 2003 Nobel Prize for literature, he lives in Adelaide, Australia.* I hadn't fully comprehended that lots of people around me in Austin not only owned guns but had them close at hand and regarded themselves as free to use them.

BILL HELMER: I remember thinking, "All we need is a bunch of idiots running around with rifles." But what they did turned out to be brilliant. Once he could no longer lean over the edge and fire, he was much more limited in what he could do. He had to shoot through those drain spouts, or he had to pop up real fast and then dive down again. That's why he did most of his damage in the first twenty minutes.

JOHN PIPKIN: I'd left Scholz's and was sitting across the street from the Chi Omega house when this Texas Ranger walked up carrying a pair of binoculars and a rifle with a scope on it. For some reason, he picked me out of the group of kids sitting on the curb. He said, "Son, you ever done any hunting?" And I said, "Yes, sir, I've been hunting all my life." He said, "Well, take these binoculars. I need for you to calibrate me." And I said, "Okay." Whitman would stick his rifle out through one of these drainpipes on the observation deck every once in a while and shoot at someone. The ranger would shoot back, and I'd say, "You're an inch too high," or "Bring it over to the left a couple inches."

BILL HELMER: A friend of mine was glued to the TV at the San Jacinto Cafe, near campus, when a guy with a deer rifle ran in, grabbed a six-pack of beer, and ran back out.

ANN MAJOR: It seemed like every other guy had a rifle. There was a sort of cowboy atmosphere, this "Let's get him" spirit.

JOHN PIPKIN: I was looking through the binoculars when all of a sudden I thought to myself, "Gosh, he's pointing that rifle at me." It was like I could see up inside the barrel of the rifle, from four hundred yards away. The next thing I knew, I could feel bullets grazing the top of the hair on my head. The ranger said, "Boy, we got his attention now." I was absolutely terrified. I dropped the binoculars and scrambled around behind a tree, and then a car. I sat there and panted, thinking how close I'd come to being shot. The ranger said, "You okay, son?" I said, "I guess. I'm alive." He said, "Yeah, that was pretty close." And I said, "Yes, sir, it was too close. I think I'm done with my spotting."

"THAT WAS THE MOMENT THAT SEPARATED THE BRAVE PEOPLE FROM THE SCARED PEOPLE."

An armored car was used to evacuate some of the victims, but many had to lie in the line of fire for an hour or longer. EMS did not exist yet; ambulances were still run by local funeral homes, and drivers did their best that afternoon to treat the injured without getting killed themselves. Many students risked their own lives to help wounded strangers like patrolman Billy Speed, who lay dying on the South Mall.

BRENDA BELL: We were holed up in Parlin Hall when Billy Speed was shot, and he was close enough that I could have thrown my pencil on him. A couple of students crept out the back door and made their way to him. A girl took off her slip and used it to try to stanch the bleeding, but he was bleeding a lot. The guy who was with her had gotten a little tin cup and filled it with water. It was just like in the cowboy movies, right? You give the guy a drink of water from a tin cup and you rip up a sheet and you try to bind the wound. That was the moment that separated the brave people from the scared people. I realized that there was no way that I was going out there to help him. I didn't want to get shot. That was a defining moment, because I realized I was a coward.

BOB HIGLEY: Clif Drummond and I wanted to see if there was anything we could do to help. We took an interior stairwell down to the bottom floor of the Texas Union and exited on the Drag. A lot of kids were standing there, hugging that west wall pretty good. Across the street was a student sitting against a parking meter, obviously wounded, his head slumped over. We later learned his name was Paul Sonntag. Nobody was going over to help him. Drummond said something to the effect of "Let's go get him." We looked each other in the eye and had a *Butch Cassidy and the Sundance Kid* kind of moment. I said, "Are you going first or am I?"

CLIF DRUMMOND: It looked like a very long way across that street at the time, I'll tell you. There was essentially abject silence except for the sound of the shooting echoing off the limestone. There was zero traffic. In fact, cars were sitting out in the middle of the Drag with their doors hanging open, motors running, no one in them.

BOB HIGLEY: Drummond led out. I went one or two steps behind him, and if he moved left, I moved more to the right, and we went straight across the Drag.

CLIF DRUMMOND: We got shot at as we crossed the street, but he missed. I remember the pavement flicking, bursting, as bullets were hitting it.

BOB HIGLEY: We got across the street and lay down behind a car for cover. We worked our way up, on our bellies, to Sonntag. Drummond felt for a pulse and couldn't find one. Sonntag's fingers were totally blue. I pulled him in close, and his head rolled over, and that's when I saw he had been hit right in the mouth. He must have heard the gunshot and turned to look over his shoulder at the Tower as he was walking down the Drag.

CLIF DRUMMOND: A person we didn't know in a station wagon—someone crazier than us—came wheeling around Twenty-fourth Street and roared to a stop in front of us. He got out and opened the rear doors and pulled out a gurney. We loaded Sonntag onto that gurney, and it was really difficult because he was deadweight. The cognition kicked in right then, and I remember thinking to myself, "This is really damned serious." We had a dead guy on our hands, and we were standing still in an open place as we loaded him in.

BOB HIGLEY: There was no zigging, no zagging to be done. We were sitting ducks. It was right then that my fear gave way to anger, just pure anger. The whole thing was so unfair. I was still thinking that Sonntag had been badly wounded, that he was capable of being resuscitated. I couldn't have gone on if I'd thought, "Gee, we just recovered the body of a dead student." I couldn't allow myself to believe that this kid was dead.

NEAL SPELCE was the news director for KTBC-TV. A retired anchorman, he lives in Spicewood. Our radio news director, Joe Roddy, went to Brackenridge Hospital and read the names off the first list of casualties. As soon as he finished, Paul Bolton, who was back in the newsroom, grabbed the microphone and said, "Joe, hold it." Bolton was the very first television news anchor in Austin, a good friend of LBJ's. He was a gruff, hard-boiled newsman, but you could hear that his voice was wavering. He said, "I think you have my grandson on there. Go over that list of names again, please." Well, his grandson was Paul Sonntag. His full name, we later found out, was Paul Bolton Sonntag— his namesake. Joe read through the list again, and Bolton pretty much broke down in the newsroom.

"THE EMERGENCY ROOM LOOKED LIKE SOMETHING YOU'D SEE IN VIETNAM."

Thirty-nine of Whitman's victims were taken to the emergency room of Brackenridge Hospital in the span of ninety minutes. The first victim arrived at 12:12 p.m., and patients continued arriving at the rate of one every two minutes for the first hour.

ROBERT HEARD: I don't remember being unloaded from the ambulance. The only thing I remember is waking up on a cot on the lower floor of Brackenridge. There was blood everywhere. The doctors and nurses were slipping as they scurried across the floor.

CAMILLE CLAY was a nursing supervisor at Brackenridge. Now retired, she lives in Austin. The emergency room looked like something you'd see in Vietnam. I had never seen anything like it in my life, and I never want to see anything like it again.

HOWARD HUGHES *was an intern at the hospital. He is a physician at the University of Texas Health Center in Austin.* The casualties came pouring in. Initially there were only ten interns, two surgical residents, and our supervisor. Many of the wounds were bleeding out quickly, so we shouted back and forth, trying to decide which patients should go to the operating rooms first and doing whatever we could to stabilize the gunshot victims. There was blood everywhere, patients in the halls, not enough operating tables or available doctors.

PATSY GERMAN *was a graduate student in history. A retired teacher, she lives in Richardson.* I remember the nauseating feeling when they kept reporting the death toll on TV. We all went to the blood bank near Brackenridge, and the lines of cars went on for what seemed like miles. Kids lined up on the median to donate blood.

CAMILLE CLAY: It was a horribly hot day. And some of the kids that had been shot and had to lie out on the cement for a while had first- and second-degree burns.

HOWARD HUGHES: Many of the victims seemed to have well-placed shots through the chest, with the exception of the pregnant lady, who was shot in the abdomen.

CLAIRE JAMES: I knew immediately that I'd lost the baby. By the eighth month, your baby's moving a lot. And after I got shot, the baby never moved.

CAMILLE CLAY: We put the victims who we believed to be deceased in one room, on the floor. You just couldn't believe it, all those dead teenagers lying on the floor. They were shoulder to shoulder, with just enough room to step between them. We started trying to identify them.

You see, they didn't come in with their wallets and purses and things. One in particular I remember was a boy who was wearing a class ring from Austin High School that was engraved with his initials. I called the principal and asked him to pull the records for the class of 1966.

ROBERT PAPE *was the hospital's director of medical education. A retired physician, he lives in Seguin.* Doctors who were experienced in trauma started arriving at the hospital and offering to do whatever needed to be done. General practitioners, psychiatrists, dermatologists came too. Fifty-eight doctors signed the ledger in the emergency room and volunteered their help.

CAMILLE CLAY: There were a lot of hysterical people trying to get into the emergency room. Finally the police had to go outside and put up a barricade.

ROBERT HEARD: The AP sent its Austin correspondent, a reporter named Garth Jones, to my hospital room. Garth Jones couldn't write home for money. But he faithfully took down the notes I gave him. He came to my room and he stood over against the wall, and I recounted what happened to me. The story was only about seven or eight inches long, but it ran around the world.

"THE SNIPER STARTED GOING DOWN . . ."

Police officer Ramiro Martinez was at home, off duty, and cooking himself a steak for lunch when he turned on the TV and saw KTBC's noon news bulletin. He immediately called in to the police department and was told by a lieutenant to find an intersection by the university where he could work traffic. Martinez put on his uniform, jumped in his 1954 Chevrolet, and drove to campus. When he saw that there were more than enough officers directing traffic away from the university, he decided to head for the Tower.

RAMIRO MARTINEZ *was a patrolman for the Austin Police Department. A retired Texas Ranger, he lives in New Braunfels.* When I reached
the South Mall, I could see people hiding behind trees and hedges.
There were wounded people, dead people, people whose conditions
I did not know lying on the sidewalk. There was a pregnant woman
who was twisting, wilting, in the hot sun. I ran as fast as I could, zig-
zagging toward the Tower, and somehow made it without getting shot.

A security guard was sitting inside, and I asked if I could borrow his
handheld radio. I tried all the channels, but I couldn't make contact
with the department. I tried the phone, but the lines were jammed;
all I got was a busy signal. At that point, I decided that I needed to
get upstairs. My training in the Army had taught me that when you
encounter a situation like this, you establish a command post right
away. Then you organize an assault team. I figured I just needed to get
upstairs and find out what the game plan was.

I got on the elevator and pressed the button for the twenty-seventh
floor. By that time I was starting to feel pretty uneasy, because I wasn't
seeing any other officers. As a Catholic, I was taught to ask the good
Lord for forgiveness if I thought my life might be in danger. And so
as I was going up in the elevator, watching those little numbers light
up, I decided to say an Act of Contrition. Then I pulled out my .38 and
pointed it at the elevator doors. I didn't know what I was going to find
when I got to the top of the Tower.

When the elevator doors opened, police officer Jerry Day and a civilian named Allen Crum were facing me holding a pistol and a rifle.
We all let out huge sighs of relief the moment we saw each other. An
officer with the Department of Public Safety's intelligence section was
sitting at a desk, dialing, trying to establish communications. The
man next to him was drawing a map of the observation deck—and
that was it. I couldn't believe it. There was no game plan. We were the
whole enchilada.

I decided to secure the floor, and I had started opening doors when
I saw a very distraught middle-aged man holding a pair of white wom-

en's shoes with blood on them. I didn't know this at the time, but he was M. J. Gabour [Michael's father]. He said, "The son of a bitch killed my family up there. Let me have your gun and I'll go kill him." He tried to grab my gun away from me, so Jerry Day and I had to restrain him. We wrestled him into the elevator, and Day took him downstairs. We couldn't afford to have any distractions.

Finally, I opened the door that led up to the observation deck. There were bloody footprints on the stairs. Knowing I had to walk up those steps was a lonely feeling. Allen Crum said, "Where are you going?" I said, "Up." He said, "Well, I'm coming with you." I didn't realize until a little while later, when he asked me to deputize him, that he wasn't a police officer, but as far as I was concerned, he had more than passed the test, and I was glad to have him with me. To say I wasn't scared would make me either a liar or a fool.

When we reached the first landing, I could see the face of a young boy. His eyes were open, looking at me, and he was dead. I advanced toward him, hugging the wall. It seemed like an eternity to get to him. I quickly looked around the corner and saw a dead woman lying at his feet. Another woman was lying there, and we turned her on her side to keep her from drowning in her own blood. There was a wounded young man who was slumped against a wall, still conscious. He said, "He's outside," and pointed upstairs.

The shooting outside sounded just like rolling thunder, and the reports of the guns down below were echoing back and forth off of the buildings. I couldn't see the sniper, so I slowly opened the glass door, a little at a time, and stepped outside. There were shell casings everywhere. Crum kept me covered while I looked around the southeast corner, but the sniper was not in sight. I told Crum to remain in his position while I went to the northeast corner. I kept down, because the bullets that civilians were firing from down below kept hitting the limestone and showering dust and little pieces of rock.

Before I reached the northeast corner, I turned and saw an officer I knew, Houston McCoy, standing behind me with a shotgun. All I had was my .38, so that shotgun looked pretty beautiful at that moment. I advanced to the northeast corner, looked around it, and that's when I saw the sniper. He was sitting about forty feet away with an M1 carbine, and he looked like he had a target in his sights. I immediately fired a round at him and hit him somewhere on his left side. He leapt to his feet and started to turn around, trying to bring his rifle down to return fire. I emptied my gun. I hollered at McCoy to fire, which he did, hitting him. The sniper started going down, and that's when I reached up—my gun was empty—and grabbed the shotgun from McCoy. I blasted him one more time as he was falling. And then it was over. He was flat on his back, and I knew he was dead.

"EVERYBODY POURED OUT OF THEIR HIDING PLACES."

The shooting ended at 1:24 p.m. Allen Crum found a towel and waved it over his head to signal that the ordeal was over. Neal Spelce, who was broadcasting live several blocks south of the Tower and whose report was playing on transistor radios across campus, said, "The sniper is dead." All told, Whitman had shot 43 people. Fifteen were dead, including his wife and his mother.

ANN MAJOR: Everybody poured out of their hiding places. It was a beautiful, sunny day, but I saw many dead people, mostly young, lying on the grass where they had been shot. Mike Cox was a copyboy at the *Austin American-Statesman*. He is a spokesman for the Texas Department of Transportation in Austin. I remember hearing the chilling sound of what surely was every siren on every ambulance in Austin.

JOHN PIPKIN: The world came alive again. Hundreds of people emerged from wherever they had been hiding. The Tower was like a magnet; everyone started walking toward it.

BILL HELMER: I was standing outside of the Academic Center when I heard a group of students yell, "Lynch the son of a bitch!" Judging from their nice haircuts and neat clothes, I judged them to be frat boys. That was the only time I heard that sort of thing.

FORREST PREECE: I was part of a huge mass of people sweeping east toward the Tower. The whole crowd was silent. No shouts, no cries for revenge—just a mass of humanity moving as one. When I had reached a spot near the steps of the Academic Center, a weird tableau of three men walking west, against the grain, parted us like the Red Sea, slowing me for a few seconds. I instantly knew who they were and what they had done—that they had killed, or somehow stopped, the shooter. In the middle was a Hispanic police officer who seemed to be in a state of shock. His uniform was soaked through, as if someone had hosed him down. His eyes were locked into the thousand-yard stare. Two men were holding him up. The man on his left was whispering soothing words to him as they walked past: "You did okay, buddy. Ease up. You did okay. It's all right."

CLIF DRUMMOND: We reached the west side of the Tower, and I had never seen that many people crammed into such a small space. I want to say there were easily a thousand people standing shoulder to shoulder. There wasn't a breeze moving in any direction, and the crowd was totally quiet. It was so hot that you could almost see the heat. There were lots of rifles—all on safety, barrels pointed up, butts resting on waistbands. You could see the barrels sticking up out of the crowd.

BRENDA BELL: We all gathered at the Tower, as if by common agreement. We wanted to take a look at the guy who did this; we wanted to see him led out in handcuffs, or dead. That was why we were there. But instead, there was this procession of bodies.

BILL HELMER: The cops brought out the dead and wounded. That was really grim: blood everywhere, heads blown apart, hands dragging on the pavement. It took fifteen or twenty minutes. They wheeled Whitman out on a stretcher—out the back, to avoid the mob. He was covered by a sheet that had gotten partly pulled back, and he was all shot to hell. He looked like bloody steak tartare.

CLIF DRUMMOND: Someone, maybe a policeman, said, "That's the shooter. They got him." There was lots of cheering when they brought the guy out.

BRENDA BELL: I walked around afterward, and there was blood everywhere. It was hot, so it had turned dark. It was on the mall, all over the sidewalk, up and down the Drag, on the carpet of Sheftall's jewelers. A lot of store windows were shot out. But it was all cleaned up very fast. One of the orders that [UT regent] Frank Erwin gave was "Clean this mess up."

SHEL HERSHORN *was a photographer for Life magazine. Now retired, he lives in Gallina, New Mexico.* I'd gotten a call in Dallas from *Life* telling me to get down to Austin. By the time I got there, Whitman was dead. I'd heard there was a foot-wide swath of blood across the carpet at Sheftall's, so I went there and started making pictures. One of those pictures ended up being the cover photo for the magazine; it was taken through the store window, which was shot up with bullet holes, looking up at the Tower. But this competing photographer had other ideas; he was pacing up and down the sidewalk outside, waiting his turn. So when I was done, I kicked the window out. The store owner came running up to me, very upset. I told him not to worry. I said, "*Life* magazine will pay for that."

BILL HELMER: At Scholz's, students were taking up donations and passing around a petition on a spread-out grocery bag thanking the ambulance drivers for their terrific work.

MIKE COX: My friend Don Vandiver and I didn't get out of the *Statesman* until after midnight. We went to campus and walked around in the dark, drinking cans of beer. We were trying to process what we had seen, trying to get drunk so we could wash it away. Lots of students were still walking around campus in amazement. I remember noticing that sand had been spread out on the concrete to soak up the blood.

"WHY DID WHITMAN DO IT?"

When an autopsy was performed on Whitman the next morning, Dr. Coleman de Chenar discovered what appeared to be a small brain tumor. The consensus in the medical community, however, was that the tumor was probably not to blame, given its size and location. (Whitman was not neurologically impaired at the time of the shootings, for example; he was a crack shot.) As for what had made him "snap," there were plenty of theories. Was it his abusive childhood? His overwhelming anger? The amphetamines he consumed, observed one friend, "like popcorn"?

JOHN ECONOMIDY: The day after the shootings, the university held a press conference in the main newsroom of the *Daily Texan*. It turned out that Whitman had gone into the Student Health Center that spring complaining of terrible headaches and depression and had seen a psychiatrist named Maurice Heatly. Heatly was the brother of a very powerful state legislator, and that caused some embarrassment politically, because—as the university, to its credit, immediately disclosed—Whitman had told him exactly what he planned to do. Heatly wrote in his report, which was released to reporters, that Whitman was "oozing with hostility" and had expressed a desire to go to the top of the Tower and shoot people with a deer rifle. That was a jaw-dropper. Heatly defended himself by saying that if he committed every kid who threatened to jump off the Tower or do harm to others, there would be a lot of people in the psychiatric ward.

NEAL SPELCE: Why did Whitman do it? [Then-governor] John Connally put together a commission to explore the question, but they couldn't find a definitive answer. There was nothing anyone could ever point to and say, "Oh, that's why." It just remained a mystery.

KINKY FRIEDMAN *had graduated in May. A singer, novelist, and 2006 independent gubernatorial candidate, he lives near Kerrville.* I wrote "The Ballad of Charles Whitman" shortly afterward. I'm sure the people who didn't like it thought I was mocking a tragedy or something, but they didn't listen to the song. It explores the mind of Charles Whitman and what makes these things happen. The question is, Why? Why would somebody do that? He was a straight-A student, an Eagle Scout, a Marine—just a good all-around, all-American asshole. I doubt if his neighbors thought he was evil. That's usually how it is: "He was not without his charm." We profess to find it deplorable, but we're fascinated because there's a little bit of Charlie in us all. We're all capable of terrible acts, and we're all capable of greatness. It's a question of which angels we're listening to, I suppose.

SHELTON WILLIAMS: The cover of *Life* the next week made a big impression on all of us. The photo, which was taken from the victim's point of view, was of the Tower, as seen through a window with two gaping bullet holes in it. From that vantage point it looked menacing, even evil—not the triumphant symbol of football victories we were used to.

FORREST PREECE: I was sitting with the rest of the Longhorn Band in Memorial Stadium at the first football game that September when [announcer] Wally Pryor asked us to remember those who had been injured. He suggested giving to the designated people who would be standing with donation cans at the exits. I remember that John Wayne was in attendance, because we were playing his alma mater, USC, and he gave a significant amount of cash. But a story in the next issue of the *Daily Texan* said that the total take was pitifully small.

A friend who was part of the collection effort said he was amazed at how quickly people seemed to forget.

BARTON RILEY: The fall semester started and life went on, just like nothing had ever happened. I never heard it mentioned. Isn't that amazing? I was rather stunned.

CLAIRE JAMES: I was in intensive care for seven weeks, and I wasn't released from the hospital until November. I had to learn how to walk again. When I went back to school in January, no one said anything to me or talked about it around me. I almost felt like I had imagined the whole thing. Not one person ever called together the students who'd been injured that day and said, "How are you?" or "We're so sorry." I guess that's just the way it was—it was a measure of the times. We didn't have the vocabulary at that point to deal with what had happened. If it was mentioned at all, it was always called "the accident."

"IT WAS LIKE AN INJURY THAT WOULD NEVER HEAL."

The observation deck was closed after the shootings and then reopened two years later. The board of regents closed it indefinitely in 1974, after a series of suicides. It reopened on September 16, 1999. In 2001 Whitman claimed another life. David Gunby, who had endured chronic kidney problems ever since he was shot in the back, elected to discontinue dialysis. The Tarrant County medical examiner ruled his death a homicide.

BRAD CRIDER *is an independent builder living in Austin.* My girlfriend, Ginger, and I live in Charlie Whitman's house. We signed the lease not knowing; our neighbor across the alleyway was the one who told me. I honestly didn't think much about it until the first day I was here. I was doing some work on the house when a couple approached me from the street and said, "Do you mind if we take a tour?" They had driven in from Houston to see where Whitman used to live. I said sure, and they were so excited you would have thought they had just won the lottery. Most people just drive by slowly and then turn around and come back for a second look. I've seen strangers taking photos of the house; my neighbors have seen people parked in front of their houses, filming from an angle so they won't be too obvious. Ginger jokes that we should put a plaque in our yard that says "Charlie Whitman doesn't live here anymore."

ROSA EBERLY *taught a course at UT called "The UT Tower and Public Memory" from 1996 to 2001. She is an associate professor of rhetoric at Penn State University, in University Park, Pennsylvania.* One of the things we looked at was how, in that institutional memory vacuum, pop culture had been able to turn Whitman into a cool antihero. He was the subject of songs and films and even a Web site created by an alum that was called the Charles Whitman Fan Club. Part of why there wasn't a memorial on campus for so long, I think, was out of concern that it would become a shrine to Whitman.

HARPER SCOTT CLARK: A bullet of Whitman's had ripped a big chunk out of one of the balustrades on the South Mall, and for the rest of the time I was at UT, whenever my friends and I would stroll by there, we would run our fingers inside it and look up at the Tower and think contemplatively. I went back years later and saw that someone had filled it in with plaster. It was gone, and I remember thinking that was a big mistake.

LARRY FAULKNER *was a graduate student in chemistry. The immediate past president of UT-Austin, he lives in Houston, where he is the president of Houston Endowment.* I had been at the university that day. Whitman opened fire moments after I walked off campus. Since that time, the university's stance had always seemed to be to try to erase what had happened, but with absolutely no success. It was like an injury that would never heal. And I instinctively felt that the way to get past that was to open the observation deck to the public again. I had that as a goal in my mind before I walked on campus as president, in 1998. I believed it was my job to place before the regents a proposal that they could support. And that meant addressing the issues that had caused them to close it in the first place; we had to have a physical barrier to prevent suicides and accidents, and we had to have a credible way of screening for weapons.

ANNIE HOLAND *was the student body president for the 1998–1999 academic year. She is the executive vice president and chief operating officer of Holand Investment, in McAllen.* Students had presented proposals to the administration year after year, but there had always been resistance until we met with Dr. Faulkner. The observation deck had been closed for so long that it had become a kind of mystical place. There were all sorts of folk tales around campus about the students who had jumped to their deaths, and Whitman, of course. It was only associated with tragedy.

LARRY FAULKNER: The university had never recognized, in any formal way, the people who had been injured that day. So we enhanced the garden behind the Tower and we dedicated it to them. We also held a memorial service, 33 years after the fact.

CHARLES LOCKE *is the tour coordinator at the Tower.* We have hour-long, student-guided tours, but the tragedy that occurred in '66 is not part of our formal presentation. The guides are encouraged to be knowledgeable about the tragedy so they can respond to questions if they are posed. Our intent is not to make this the "Charles Whitman tour," because that's not the reason, we hope, that people visit the Tower. One of the benefits of reopening the Tower is that we can reclaim it as a symbol of academic excellence represented by the university.

BOB HIGLEY: I can't look at the Tower without thinking of that day. It dominates the silhouette of the city. I love it when we're number one and they make it orange; that's a kick for me. But that's always at night, in the dark. During the day, if I see the Tower, I'm carried back. I think about how Paul Sonntag was eighteen years old when he died. And the week before August 1, and the week after, I think about it night after night.

CLIF DRUMMOND: I'm a country boy, and so I had always loved to go to the Tower. It was a high place, and we don't have high places in West Texas. When you got up there, it was calm and cool, and you could see for a long ways. You could see all over campus, all over this beautiful city, way out to the Hill Country. People went up there all the time. And Charles Whitman ruined that. He took it away from us. It may sound trivial, but he took that away.

2

"I Dream About It Every Night": What Happens to Americans Who Film Police Violence

BY OLIVER LAUGHLAND AND JON SWAINE

Feidin Santana relives the morning of Saturday 4 April 2015 on a near continuous loop. It was around 9.30am and the 23-year-old was running uncharacteristically late for work. As he walked his usual route through the back streets of North Charleston, something caught his eye: a black man running away from a white police officer.

Santana followed the chase for a few yards to a deserted patch of lawn behind a pawn shop and a car dealership. Here the officer caught up with the man, and ended up on top of him. Watching from behind a chainlink fence, Santana instinctively reached for his phone and pressed record.

The morning was still, silent. "You could hear birds flying, the swing of their wings," Santana says as he stands, three months later, where he was that day. "You could hear everything; the sounds of the officer, the gunshots. Everything."

Santana had hoped he might be noticed. "I believed my presence would prevent something," he says softly, his voice almost drowned by the hum of cicadas. "But it didn't happen that way."

Instead, Santana's steady hand captured the moment the unarmed, 50-year-old man, Walter Scott, broke away from the officer, Michael Slager, and attempted to flee. The officer paused for a moment, pointed his gun and fired about eight rounds until Scott lay face down on the ground.

"Everything happened too fast," Santana says. "I never imagined he'd pull his gun out. There was no way out. He [Scott] was running slow."

In the grainy footage, Slager can be seen opening fire, then walking over to Scott's body, yanking his floppy arms and placing them in handcuffs.

"Oh shit," Santana can be heard whispering, as he follows the officer. Slager jogs back to the site he fired from, picks up an object from the floor – perhaps his Taser – and drops it next to the body as another officer arrives. "Fucking abuse," Santana mutters. The two officers gaze down on Scott's corpse, seemingly oblivious to the fact that they are being filmed. Santana moves right up to the fence as Slager places his finger on Scott's neck, checking for a pulse.

The grassy patch where Scott fell is peaceful now. Memorials have been removed, and Santana looks at the ground, hands in his pockets, his lean body framed by the fence he filmed through just a few months earlier. "This is the place where everything changed," the Dominican migrant says.

Once Santana's footage went public, Slager was arrested and charged with murder. Santana's split-second decision that day marked a turning point in a new civil rights movement in the US, one born on the streets of Ferguson, Missouri, in August 2014. Then, it was 18-year-old Michael Brown who was fatally shot by officer Darren Wilson. The final few minutes of Brown's life had been captured by a small surveillance camera rolling inside a nearby grocery shop, where Brown had stolen a box of cigars before walking out with a friend. After the shooting, one of his neighbors used his phone to film Brown's bloodied body lying in the road. "They said he had his hands up and everything," the young man was recorded saying, as a crowd gathered in the midday sun.

But the violent 90-second encounter between these two recordings, which would unleash months of civil unrest on America's streets and return a dispute over race and criminal justice to the forefront of its politics, somehow eluded phone cameras. "I just wish we could have had solid proof," says Leslie McSpadden, Brown's uncle.

As protesters have taken to the streets to demonstrate over Brown's death, even a year on, so a legion of amateur cameramen and women have begun watching officers closely, posting recordings that undermine the monopoly once held by police on the official version of events. Footage of fatal encounters with police has already helped secure murder charges, not just against Slager but also against an officer in Baltimore, Maryland, who drove the police van in which Freddie Gray, a black 25-year-old, suffered fatal injuries in April – apparently contradicting official narratives filed by officers. A white police officer lost his job within days of being filmed aggressively handling teenagers outside a pool party in Texas in June. The case was cited as proof of what campaigners argue is a policing system sharply biased against African Americans, sometimes with deadly consequences.

But the surge in vigilante recording is being met with aggressive resistance from police. Judges uphold the right of American people to film law enforcement officers under the first amendment of the US constitution, and lawmakers in several states have proposed new laws specifically protecting such recording. But officers increasingly complain that filming interferes with their duties, and insist that short clips don't tell the full story of controversial encounters. An increasing number are taking direct action to prevent recordings – snatching or smashing phones or demanding the handover of footage, sometimes even after it has been livestreamed directly online.

For many who capture horrific acts of violence, returning to a normal life becomes impossible. They complain of harassment by police, of threats against their life and of recurring trauma as a result of the death and brutality they have witnessed.

In the barber shop where he works, in a dusty strip mall by a motorway, Santana is friendly, relaxed. But walking to the site where Scott was killed, his mood shifts; he talks slowly, pausing and casting his eyes into the distance. "I try not to come back here," he says. "But you cannot ignore your fears. Sometimes I cross by. I look at the video and I see myself, how everything happened."

Santana migrated to America with his family 10 years ago, at 13. Like many who come to the US from Latin America, he arrived without a word of English, in pursuit of a better life. He has, he says, lived a "nomadic existence", moving from city to city in his late teens; spending a short time back in the Dominican Republic, playing shortstop in the baseball Prospect League, hoping to be scouted by a major league club in the US. But he injured his shoulder and moved alone to North Charleston in 2013 to start a career as a barber, sending money back home to his wife and one-year-old son.

He describes himself as someone who "gets along with everybody". But adds, "I'm a person who doesn't like injustice." It was this that informed his decision to follow Scott and Slager that day, and guided his actions after he turned the camera off.

As officers began to swarm around Scott's body, Santana shouted and told one he had witnessed the entire event. "I told him what happened was an abuse, and that I had it on record," he recalls. The officer told him to stay where he was but then, inexplicably, he was allowed to leave the crime scene. He feared officers might seize his phone and the footage would be lost forever, so he took flight.

"I just left, right in front of their eyes. They didn't try to stop me. I don't know why." He wasn't certain if the film had saved and as he ran to the barber's shop he looked back at his handset. The footage was there. "I couldn't believe it recorded . . . I got nervous, I tried to send it to another phone."

But he quickly decided against sharing it with anyone, worried about how it might be handled. The gravity of what he had just witnessed began to sink in. At this point, Santana's close friend Tawayne Weems walked into the barber's shop.

Weems, 43, is assistant principal at the local high school. An African American who speaks fluent Spanish, he met Santana when he first moved to North Charleston. Weems quickly became a father figure to him, helping him establish himself in a city where he had no family.

But on that day back in April, the two had not seen each other in months. Weems had popped by to get a haircut, and describes the moment he saw the footage: "We went outside, he showed it to me in the car. I knew this was on the precipice of something big, that could really change things," he says. "But initially I didn't want to get involved."

The two watched the news that afternoon, which led with a story on Scott's death. To their shock, the reports reproduced the official lie: that Scott had been shot after he grabbed Slager's Taser and the officer feared for his life. "Then it was like, well, we got to say something," Weems says. They vowed to get the video to Scott's family.

Santana later shared a copy with his wife in the Dominican Republic, under strict instructions that if anything were to happen to him, she should send it only to Weems. He feared for his life: "You're scared of who you're dealing with. You know it's law enforcement, who are meant to be doing their job, but then they're saying the opposite of what you saw. It goes through your mind . . . what could happen next? I'm the only one with the evidence."

That evening Santana contacted a local protester who had led a rally in support of the Scott family, sending him a screenshot of his footage over Facebook. The next afternoon, at a vigil, the activist introduced him to Scott's brother, Anthony. As Santana played the video from his phone, Anthony broke down in tears. But still Santana held on to it: he wanted his own attorney in place before he handed it over on Monday.

By Tuesday evening, the video was playing on every US news channel and, later, around the world. Santana stood in the barber shop and watched a press conference held by North Charleston's mayor, who announced that Slager had been charged with murder. Then Santana heard the question he'd been dreading: a journalist asked who had filmed the video.

"That's when I really got scared. When something you have done is on national TV, worldwide TV," he says, "you have to live through that to understand it."

It is a fear that Ramsey Orta, a New York City resident and also 23, understands only too well. Orta filmed the death of Eric Garner, capturing the moment the 43-year-old was placed in a banned chokehold by an NYPD officer and uttered his last words: "I can't breathe."

Lawyers Ken Perry and William Aronin sit in the poky downtown Manhattan apartment that serves as their office. The pair, separated in age by over three decades, make up Orta's legal team.

"We don't discuss where Ramsey is now, for obvious reasons, other than to say he is in the city and with family," says Aronin, 31.

Orta no longer gives interviews and will not disclose his location. "I'm still happy I took the video," he said in a statement via his lawyers. "I just wish I was able to keep my name out of it."

Orta had a criminal past before the Garner incident, including convictions for drugs sales and possession of stolen property. But since the video emerged a year ago, he has endured three stints in New York's notorious Rikers Island jail. His lawyers argue that he has been the subject of a targeted campaign at the hands of the NYPD. They list what they claim are deficiencies in the criminal cases pending against their client, which consist of two recent drug dealing charges and a weapons possession charge that occurred just two weeks after the Garner video emerged.

"He's basically a whistleblower," Aronin says. "Two weeks after he blows the whistle on horrific police abuse, the police just happen to find him waving a gun in plain sight. It's ridiculous."

Perry argues that the DNA evidence on the gun charge is inconclusive, and says of video evidence turned over in Orta's first drugs case, "You can't see shit, you can't hear shit."

The NYPD did not respond to a request for comment about the pending cases, but Orta is due to stand trial later in the year.

Orta is not the only witness to have gone to ground. Kevin Moore filmed the moment 25-year-old Freddie Gray was bundled into the back of a police van in Baltimore, minutes before he sustained a horrific spinal injury that later killed him. Moore, 28, was arrested days after Gray's death, after a protest in the city. He was released without charge, but described the incident as a deliberate act of intimidation. He has not been heard from in weeks, according to local activists.

Perhaps unsurprisingly, leading law enforcement figures have tried to play down the legitimacy of these clips. Bill Bratton, New York's veteran police commissioner, accuses activists of exploiting a handful of regrettable cases "to try to define American policing". With physical altercations, he says, "It's lawful – but it looks awful."

Earlier this year, Jason Villalba, a Republican representative in the Texas legislature, became the latest US politician to propose new laws banning people from filming police. Until last year, recording officers in Illinois without permission was a felony crime punishable by up to 15 years in prison. Efforts during the last legislative sessions to pass laws protecting the right to film failed in Connecticut, Mississippi and Montana.

But a steadily growing weight of opinion holds that filming the police is legal. Courts in Illinois and Massachusetts have ruled that filming is protected by the first amendment of the US constitution, and the US supreme court declined in 2012 to consider an appeal against the Massachusetts decision, meaning the nation's highest court turned down an opportunity to restrict filming across the country. Villalba withdrew his bill amid a crescendo of criticism just days after the emergence of Santana's footage in South Carolina, and laws protecting filmers were enacted during the last sessions in Arkansas, Colorado and Oregon.

But Ron Hosko, a former senior FBI official, cautions that a black hand-held phone could easily be mistaken for a gun by police officers having to make split-second decisions under intense pressure. "This is not a time to be engaged in a frolic," he says. "The police sometimes shoot and kill people who turn out not to have something."

Chuck Canterbury, national president of the Fraternal Order of Police, adds that filming often hinders officers trying to do their jobs. "People are interfering by getting much too close," he says.

Both Hosko and Canterbury claim many clips are misleadingly edited. They decry the treatment of Eric Casebolt, the police officer who resigned amid widespread criticism after he was filmed manhandling a black girl and pointing his gun at two black boys outside a pool party in McKinney, a Dallas suburb. The footage, recorded on a mobile phone by a 15-year-old, dominated the national media after sweeping across the internet.

"You only get what the person who filmed it wants you to see," Canterbury says of amateur footage. "The McKinney video did not show the facilitating incident, the fights taking place, the residents who were demanding police action."

"One thing is for sure in America," Hosko says of the two unarmed boys who approached Casebolt before he drew his weapon. "You're rolling up to a potential gun fight, because at least one person has a gun. You may have a gun in your face."

Both men support efforts to restrict filming to a set distance away from officers, or to outlaw interference with police fulfilling their duties.

When Mekkel Richards and Adam Malinowski saw eight police officers pushing a man to the ground and beating him in downtown

Detroit one evening last summer, both reached for their phones. The two students had been walking back from a fireworks display. Standing three meters apart, they watched the scene as their digital cameras rolled, blood seeping from the man's head.

"That's when I realized that what we've all read about and seen on the TV about police brutality is real, and not a rarity," says Richards, who is 23.

Soon they were spotted. "Get the fuck back," Richards says one officer told him. "Put your phone away, you can't be videotaping," said another. One pushed him to the ground, he says, and when he stood up, another officer punched him in the face.

Realizing Malinowski was recording this, too, the officer ran towards him and placed him in a headlock before slamming him to the ground and handcuffing him, he alleges. The officers smashed Malinowski's iPhone and erased recordings on Richards's device, the pair say. "I've never felt as threatened as I did that day," Malinowski says.

They were arrested, charged with interfering and had to spend the night in cells. They claim one officer told them they were "faggot tree huggers that take the whole rights thing too seriously". Malinowski had his case dismissed following probation. The case against Richards was dismissed when police did not turn up to court.

The two men recently filed a lawsuit accusing the officers and their city bosses of assault, false imprisonment, malicious prosecution and violating their constitutional rights. "It's unfortunate the only way to hold police accountable legally for this is to sue them for money," says Malinowski, who is now 22.

Their case was the most violent in a series of recent confrontations, according to Carlos Miller, a former journalist who now tracks the issue on his website, Photography Is Not A Crime. Already this year, the site has reported on 87 cases in which people were arrested, manhandled or threatened for filming police. The rate of such incidents has increased in recent years, Miller says. "It's great we have all these laws, but the battle continues. We're not going to back down, and nor are they."

In June, an officer in Austin, Texas, was filmed snatching the phone of a man recording the police, then pepper-spraying him. The previous month in North Carolina, a man was arrested and charged with interfering while filming his friend being arrested. "How do you stop your phone?" an officer can be heard asking on his footage.

In March in New Jersey, Phillip White was filmed being mauled by a police dog, in an incident that led to his death. One officer approached the bystander who had been recording and, after confirming he had captured the entire thing, told him: "I'm going to take your phone." The footage was later obtained by a local TV news station.

In a bid to counter the backlash from officers, a number of developers have created automatic mobile video upload software. One such app, released by the New York Civil Liberties Union in 2012, at the height of the NYPD's use of "stop and frisk", sends recorded footage straight to a legal observer at the union, effectively safeguarding recordings before they can be deleted. It has been downloaded by 35,000 city residents and tens of thousands of submissions have been received.

The videos, says Jennifer Carnig, a spokeswoman for the NYCLU, provided an unprecedented insight into discriminatory policing under stop and frisk: verbal and physical abuse, heavy-handed searches and the drawing of weapons on people who appear to be unarmed. The app also revealed new methods officers are using to stop bystanders filming them, for example by shining torches or the high beams of their patrol cars into the camera lens.

The "mobile justice" app has now been rolled out in seven other states, including California, where more than 150,000 people have downloaded it. It has yet to bring about any litigation, Carnig says, "but I think what we have gotten is this public conversation".

While one officer wheeled her chair inside the station, another loaded her into an SUV. She was taken inside and eventually charged with assaulting a police officer. She insists she has no idea what she is supposed to have done. "If I tried to hit somebody, I would dislocate something," said De Mian, who has Ehlers-Danlos syndrome, a disorder of the body's connective tissue.

De Mian got into livestreaming when her BlackBerry was knocked from her hand as she photographed riot police at a demonstration following the acquittal in July 2013 of George Zimmerman, from criminal charges over his killing of Trayvon Martin, a black 17-year-old, in Florida. She was eventually sentenced to 20 hours of community service for failure to obey a reasonable police order, after not dispersing when police declared the assembly illegal.

During the months of protests in Ferguson, she captured police pepper-spraying and tear-gassing crowds, and roughly snatching people for arrest in targeted raids. While the cable news cameras stayed back, she broadcast direct from the frontlines, sending images of the chaotic clashes to laptops all over the world.

The Obama administration's view on those who have filmed in Ferguson was unambiguous. "As the ability to record police activity has become more widespread," said a Department of Justice report, "the role it can play in capturing questionable police activity, and ensuring that the activity is investigated and subject to broad public debate, has become clear."

At Scott's funeral, a week after his death, hundreds lined up in the rain to pay their final respects. They swayed in time as a soloist sang rousing gospel, then bowed their heads in prayer. Pastor George D. Hamilton delivered a sermon, describing Santana's actions as the will of God: that he was able to "video every detail so no man could question the guilt of that murderer". As Scott's body lay surrounded by flowers, Hamilton's advice to the congregation was clear: "Keep your phone handy, keep your charge up. You never know when you need to be around."

Santana was not present at the funeral, but he was there when South Carolina's governor signed the first statewide law requiring law enforcement officers to wear body cameras. It was pushed through in the wake of the Scott incident and would not have happened without Santana's footage.

As Santana prods at his dinner, he hints at the stress that has continued since his brief exposure in the media and ahead of a likely appearance as a witness in Slager's murder trial. He moved from his home, close to the site of the shooting, after it happened. Now he moves between locations, "to be safe, to be around people you know care".

"It is something you can't ignore, something you can't erase," he says of Scott's death. "I dream about this, the same thing every single night."

He talks of the paranoia that arose after the mass shooting two months after Scott's death at a black church in Charleston, a few miles away, where a 21-year-old white supremacist is accused of murdering nine parishioners at a prayer service.

"There are many things in this state that I didn't know the real face of," he says. "After those threats, it shows you."

There is a Death to Feidin Santana Facebook group that proclaims, "He put a good man behind bars!" Has he received any direct threats?

Santana pauses and drops his eyes. "A little bit of everything, that's all I can say. I used to work from eight in the morning until 11 at night. Now I can't. I don't feel comfortable staying in the barber shop. It's not the same. I used to be there by myself, now I have to be surrounded by people." Yet he has no regrets and shrugs at the suggestion that his acts were heroic. "I believe we are here to be each other's keepers, to protect each other. I don't see anything special in what I did."

3

A Lynch Mob of One

BY IBRAM X. KENDI

Everyone seemed to be fleeing the brutality of the Chicago sun. There was no haven that compared to the cooling waters of Lake Michigan. Thousands of blacks and whites flocked to its beaches. That is where 17-year-old Eugene Williams and his friends fled. They knew all about the racial battles at the 29th Street Beach—or, they did not.

The boys splashed into the black side of the lake. Williams climbed on a raft and floated, his friends not far away. His raft accidentally drifted past the invisible color line at 29th Street onto the "whites only" side. Yes, Jim Crow had become national.

Twenty-four-year-old George Stauber saw Williams and started pummeling the boys with stones. Hit, Williams plunged into Lake Michigan and drowned. Daniel Callaghan, a Chicago police officer, arrived on the scene first and refused to arrest Stauber, as William Middleton, a black detective sergeant, insisted he should. Callaghan's backup arrived and stood as stone-faced as the stone that murdered Williams. A standoff. One black beachgoer drew a gun and fired at the police line.

Then the city's white rage, to use Carol Anderson's term, exploded amid the false rumors of a black "invasion" to "clean out" white neighborhoods. When the lynch mobs finally disassembled nearly a week later, 38 people—23 black, 15 white—had perished, more than 350 people had reported injuries, and about 1,000 black homes lay in ashes. The worst incident of white-supremacist terror during the Red Summer of 1919 ended on August 3.

Exactly a century later, on Saturday, 21-year-old Patrick Crusius, wielding an assault rifle, allegedly entered a Walmart in El Paso, Texas, and murdered 22 people. Hours later, 24-year-old Connor Betts, holding an AR-15-style firearm, allegedly entered Dayton's Oregon District and murdered nine people. A manifesto linked to Crusius said he targeted Latino people. Six of Betts's nine victims were African American in majority-white Dayton, although police have been unable to determine whether his victims were deliberately targeted.

The American crisis of white-supremacist terrorism—its deadliest form, mass murder—is as old as it is new. The death knell still sounds. The deliverer of mass death has changed.

In 1919, the white lynch mob was the deadliest domestic form of white-supremacist terror. Back then a sizable number of armed and coordinated white supremacists were needed to slaughter a sizable number of people of color. Now it takes only one.

The lynch mob endures in a different form. The assault rifle is the lynch mob of one.

Eugene Williams escaped the brutality of the Chicago sun, but, like countless Americans before and after him, he could not escape the brutality of white-supremacist terrorism. As false rumors of the black "invasion" spread, the white lynch mobs and their terror grew to "defend" their Chicago.

Southern migrants doubled Chicago's black population in the five years leading up to 1919. Racist whites despised the demographic shifts, all the black people supposedly infesting the city's historically white workforce and voting rolls. Months before the so-called Chicago race riot, black voters had put their preferred candidate over the top in the heated mayoral election.

The great northern migration of black people was cast as an invasion then, just as the great northern migration of Latino people is cast as an invasion today. The "New Negro" stood for "absolute and unequivocal social equality" then, just as the New Antiracist stands for absolute and unequivocal racial equity today. Angry and fearful whites marched with the Ku Klux Klan then, just as angry and fearful whites flock to the rallies of Donald Trump today. On Memorial Day 1927, 1,000 white-robed Klansmen marched through the neighborhood where I would grow up six decades later—Jamaica, Queens. Trump's father, Fred Trump, was arrested for "refusing to disperse from a parade." The Klansmen claimed to be defending their white supremacy.

In 1919, black people had to defend themselves all year long from white lynch mobs in more than two dozen cities across the country. The first white lynch mob that year tipped off in April in Jenkins County, Georgia, due to "a deep-seated envy and animosity toward a few thrifty and industrious Negroes," according to a local black paper. But most of the lynch mobs rose up during that Red Summer of 1919. The lynch mob, today, is again reddening an American summer.

Americans should shudder at the thought of an assault rifle in the hands of a white supremacist as they shudder at the memory of the lynch mobs of white supremacists. The carnage of yesterday is today—and it seems never ending. Lynch mobs terrorized Americans for nearly 100 years. How long will these new lynch mobs of one terrorize Americans?

Moved by the victims of gun violence, antiracists are struggling, unsuccessfully, to ban the assault rifle today and control the flow of guns—just as they struggled, unsuccessfully, to ban the lynch mob a century ago. Moved by the National Rifle Association, racists are struggling, successfully, to defend the assault rifle today as they struggled, successfully, to defend the lynch mob a century ago.

The U.S. House of Representatives passed the Dyer Anti-Lynching Bill in 1922, just as in February of 2019, the House passed H.R. 8 to enact universal background checks for all gun purchases. But filibustering segregationist senators blocked anti-lynching legislation for decades, while today Senate Majority Leader Mitch McConnell is blocking H.R. 8 from receiving a vote despite overwhelming bipartisan support.

No one in Chicago's lynch mobs wrote a manifesto to explain an attack in 1919. If someone had, then it would have resembled the manifesto linked to Crusius. "This attack is a response to the Hispanic invasion of Texas. They are the instigators, not me," it said. "I am simply defending my country from cultural and ethnic replacement brought on by an invasion." Swapping out *Hispanic* for *black* and *Texas* for *Chicago*, the 1919 manifesto would have read: "This attack is a response to the black invasion of Chicago. They are the instigators, not me."

The lynch mob of many and the lynch mob of one are formed of the same racist logic. Protect white supremacy. Crusius wrote at length about "losing Texas and a few other states with heavy Hispanic population to the Democrats," which would allow them "to win nearly every presidential election." Senator Ben "Pitchfork" Tillman defended the lynch mob on the floor of the U.S. Senate on March 23, 1900. "We of the South have never recognized the right of the negro to govern white men, and we never will. We have never believed him to be the equal of the white man."

At the time, lynch mobs were snatching the political and economic power of African Americans, justifying the carnage by also claiming, "We will not submit to [the Negro's] lust on our wives and daughters without lynching him," as Tillman did in the same speech. But as the anti-lynching crusader Ida B. Wells had already written in *Southern Horrors: Lynch Law in All Its Phases*: "Nobody in this section of the country believes the old threadbare lie that Negro men rape white women."

The threadbare lie energizing the lynch mob today is that the Latinos are invading, the Muslims are terrorizing, the Jews are exploiting, and the blacks are infesting—the threadbare lie of Trumpism is that these groups "will hasten the destruction of our country," to use the El Paso shooter's words. Instead of viewing these threadbare lies on the big screen through *The Birth of a Nation*, which was shown at the White House in 1915, the potential lynch mobs of one are viewing them on the little screen, watching Fox News, which is shown at the White House today.

Instead of reading these threadbare lies in Madison Grant's 1916 bestseller, *The Passing of the Great Race*—later translated into German, after which it found a fan in Adolf Hitler—the potential lynch mob is reading them on 8chan and other online klaverns. Less than an hour before the carnage in El Paso, the manifesto linked to Crusius was uploaded to 8chan's unmoderated message board with a request: "Do your part and spread this brothers!"

Today as yesterday, the state does little to crack down on the institutional and actual public bodies promulgating racist ideas. Then and now, the state calls the peal of white supremacy "free speech." Democrats defend the freedom of public officials to broadcast this speech with the First Amendment as vociferously as Republicans defend the freedom to buy assault rifles with the Second Amendment. Democrats blast Republicans, even as they ignore that contradiction.

A century ago, the state hardly ever investigated and cracked down on white supremacists bound to become lynch mobs, because that would mean investigating the Klan-dominated party of the Klan-adoring president of the United States, Woodrow Wilson. Today, "the FBI is hamstrung in trying to investigate the white supremacist movement," says Dave Gomez, who formerly supervised terrorism cases at the bureau. "There's some reluctance among agents to bring forth an investigation that targets what the president perceives as his base."

But there are importance differences between the old lynch mob of many and today's lynch mob of one. Police officers and public officials do not customarily participate in today's lynch mob like they used to. Tillman participated prominently in the Hamburg and Ellenton massacres in South Carolina during the violent election year of 1876. Future Chicago Mayor Richard Daley allegedly joined the white lynch mobs in Chicago in 1919.

Back then, law-enforcement officers looked away from, if they didn't participate in, the mass murder of bodies and economic lives. Their implicit sanction upped the death toll and the amount of stolen black wealth. Breaking black bodies was not, in practice, breaking the law. It was a time when "anybody white could take your whole self for anything that came to mind," to quote from Toni Morrison's masterwork, Beloved. None of the white attackers in Chicago in 1919 were ever punished.

But Betts was quickly killed by Dayton law enforcement. Crusius was apprehended and charged with capital murder, and Texas is seeking the death penalty. When the lynch mob of one fires on Americans these days, law enforcement usually responds as swiftly as it can to stop the slaughter, arresting or even killing the perpetrator. Today's lynch mob usually meets the stone face of justice. That is the hopeful news, the antiracist progress in all of this slaughter.

Today's one-man lynch mob is easier to stop. But it is harder to prevent than the old lynch mob of many. That is the disheartening news, the racist progress in all of this slaughter.

Empowered by the Ku Klux Klan Act of 1871, President Ulysses S. Grant sent federal marshals and troops into South Carolina to break up the Klan. The Klan requires the coordinated acts of many individuals to be a ready-made lynch mob. Coordinating lines can be cut. Financial resources can be seized. Leaders can be arrested. Meetinghouses can be raided.

Today, no white-supremacist organization is needed for a ready-made lynch mob. No false rumor is needed. There is no need to assemble a large group of coordinated white supremacists. Any young white male can become enraged listening to Trump's racist ideas, or reading the racist messages on 8chan. Any young white male can become the raging lynch mob, the next Crusius. All that's needed is an assault rifle, and the assault rifle of racist ideas—two weapons of war manufactured, offered for sale, and bought legally and easily in the United States of America.

With racist ideas so widespread, with so many Americans in denial about racist ideas, with "Send her back" chants so audible, with guns more numerous than people, it is hard to know when to raise a red flag on family members and ask a judge to seize their guns. State-level red-flag laws have reduced gun-related suicides—an acute problem among white males—but not necessarily mass murders.

It is hard to know who will be the lynch mob until he pulls the trigger. And the lynch mob is so instant these days. A minute later, a dozen people, including him, can be dead.

The lynch mob of one is harder to prevent than the lynch mob of many, but it is not impossible to prevent. Preventing today's lynch mob involves removing the assault rifle from his hands *and* the rifle of racist ideas from his mind.

Take the case of the El Paso shooter. Crusius lamented the economic and political power of corporate America—its unchecked march to automate. "My whole life I have been preparing for a future that currently doesn't exist. The job of my dreams will likely be automated." But if he had learned to be antiracist, then he would have realized the great truth in America's racial and economic history—that the racial polarization of the working classes has disempowered people like him and empowered the very "elites that run corporations" he so loathes.

If he had learned to be antiracist, then he would notice how immigration actually boosts wages and creates more jobs (and as a white male, he'd be at the front of the line to benefit). Indeed, the job of his dreams in Texas would have likely been the result of the very Latino immigrants he wanted to mass murder. Being racist suspended him from reality, and he ended up targeting his own livelihood in targeting Latino immigrants. Being antiracist brings Americans back to reality.

As an antiracist, he could have banded together with Latino Americans in the same social movement, in the same political party, fought with them for corporate regulations and more worker power, fought with them for the right to organize unions, and wielded those unions, parties, and movements instead of the assault rifle to achieve economic security, to save the people of the state and country he claims to love.

Antiracism and banning assault rifles could have saved Crusius—and most important, his 22 precious victims. If we are not struggling to ban and seize every assault rifle in America, if we are not struggling to control the flow of guns, if we are not promoting antiracism, if we are not striving to be antiracist ourselves, then what the hell are we doing in our lives to save life?

Banning assault rifles is literally a life-or-death conversation. So too is antiracism. Racism is death. Antiracism is life.

4

Armed Abusers

RACHEL GRABER, *Director of Public Policy*
at the National Coalition Against Domestic Violence
AND ROBERTA VALENTE, *Policy Consultant*
at the National Coalition Against Domestic Violence

INTRODUCTION

Domestic violence is endemic in America and around the world. Tens of millions of Americans experience physical violence, sexual violence, or stalking perpetrated by an intimate partner annually;[1] often, this abuse involves the use of firearms. One in three women and one in four men in the United States experience intimate partner physical violence, sexual violence, or stalking in their lifetimes.[2] Although people of all genders experience intimate partner violence, 85 percent of intimate partner violence is perpetrated by men against women.[3] Moreover, approximately half of both men and women experience psychological aggression by an intimate partner in their lifetimes.[4]

The National Coalition Against Domestic Violence defines domestic violence (used interchangeably with intimate partner violence in this chapter unless otherwise noted) as "the willful intimidation, physical assault, battery, sexual assault, and/or other abusive behavior as part of a systematic pattern of power and control perpetrated by one intimate partner against another."[5] Other abusive behaviors include psychological and emotional abuse, economic and financial abuse, stalking, threats of harm to self or others, and isolating survivors from their friends, families, and other support systems. Domestic violence is not always physical.

> "My mom, Sandy, depending on the day, was beaten for being too pretty, too ugly, too smart, too dumb, too black. This man beat my mother's limbs and down her spirit. His abuse was the deepest of betrayals. He tried to permanently rob her of her dignity, her hope, her joy, her capacity to love and receive love." —Representative Ayanna Pressley, serving the 7th District of Massachusetts, on the floor of the House of Representatives[6]

Intimate partner violence does not necessarily end when a survivor leaves a relationship. Survivors are at the greatest risk of escalating violence, including homicide, particularly with firearms, when they first reach out for help, whether the outreach be to family members, friends, victim service providers, or the criminal-legal system. Leaving an abusive relationship is not a guarantee of safety.

THE INTERSECTION BETWEEN DOMESTIC VIOLENCE AND FIREARMS:

Domestic violence and firearms are inextricably linked. Abusers use firearms as a tool by which to gain, exert, and maintain power and control over victims. Abusers threaten to use firearms to kill the victim, the victim's family members, beloved pets, friends, co-workers, community members, and themselves. An estimated 4.5 million American women alive today have been directly threatened by an abuser, and, of these, an estimated one million have either been shot or shot at.[7] A survey of callers to the Domestic Violence Hotline found that, of respondents whose abusers had access to firearms, two-thirds believed their abusers were capable of killing them.[8]

> "[He] never fired the pistol, but he would sit on my chest and point it at my head. He would put it right next to my temple." —Anonymous caller to the National Domestic Violence Hotline[9]

Even if the abuser does not have a firearm, threats to obtain a firearm in order to cause harm are a powerful tool with which to control the victim. Moreover, access to firearms is associated with more severe physical abuse, even when a firearm is not involved in the abuse.[10]

> "I lived in a house with a man that should not have had access to a gun," Dingell said in a floor speech that began after midnight Wednesday. "I know what it is like to see a gun pointed at you and wonder if you were going to live. And I know what it is like to hide in the closet and pray to God, 'Do not let anything happen to me.'" —Representative Debbie Dingell, speaking of her father during a sit-in in the House of Representatives[11]

Firearms are also used to injure and kill. Homicide is the second-leading cause of death among young women in the US.[12] Approximately one third of homicides of women ("femicides") are committed by current or former intimate partners,[13] and most intimate partner femicides are committed using firearms.[14] This may in part be due to the unique lethality of firearms; victims are twelve times more likely to survive a homicide attempt by other methods than they are to survive a homicide attempt with a firearm.[15] Moreover, research has shown that an abuser's firearm access is a significant risk factor for severe violence and death—an abuser's access to firearms increase the risk of femicide five-fold.[16] In 2015, 35 percent of women murdered by men were killed by domestic abusers with firearms.[17]

Abusers frequently target not only their victims but also the victims' loved ones, including family members, friends, pets, colleagues, and members of the community. In addition to the primary targeted victims, 20 percent of people killed in intimate partner homicides represent collateral deaths.[18] Firearm use increases the risk of homicide of multiple victims.[19]

> "Suddenly her eyes got this big because she saw him approaching with the gun. And I have tried and tried and tried to get that image out of my head because she saw him before I did. And when I turned to see what she was seeing, is when, shots rang. And it's just strange that you're that angry, and you loved us, and you could do this."[20] —Elizabeth, whose husband shot her and killed her daughter, in an interview with Amnesty International.

After decreasing for many years,[21] intimate partner homicide has recently begun to increase. This increase is due entirely to homicides committed with firearms.[22] Intimate partner homicide using means other than firearms continues to decline, but the increase in intimate partner homicides committed with firearms has been so substantial as to increase the rate overall.

Most domestic violence is committed by men against women, including intimate partner femicide by firearm. Intimate partner homicide committed by women against men is far more rare than intimate partner femicide, and as such has not been the subject of as much research. However, research does show that most intimate partner homicides committed by women against men do not involve firearms.[23] Similarly, the limited research on same-sex intimate partner homicides finds such homicides are rare and are not typically committed with firearms.[24]

FEDERAL PROHIBITORS

Many people assume that only persons convicted of felony crimes and persons who have been involuntarily committed for psychiatric care are prohibited from possessing firearms under federal law. In fact, there are nine categories of people who are restricted from possessing firearms by federal law.[25] These nine categories are typically referred to as "prohibitors"; the two most recently enacted specifically address people found by a court to be domestic abusers.

The first prohibitor, found at 18 U.S.C. 922(g)(8), was part of the original Violence Against Women Act in 1994. This provision prohibits people subject to qualifying domestic violence protective orders (DVPO)[26] from possessing firearms. Courts issue DVPOs based on evidence presented by the person seeking the protective order (the "petitioner") and, in the case of a final DVPO, the person against whom the protective order is against (the "respondent"). Survivors often seek DVPOs as a first step when leaving abusive relationships, when they are at greatest risk of escalating violence. As with seven of the other eight prohibitors, the DVPO prohibitor includes an official use exemption—respondents to protective orders are allowed to possess firearms while on duty if necessary to fulfill their duty while employed by a government agency.[27]

The second prohibitor was passed into law two years later, in 1996, and is commonly referred to as the "Lautenberg Amendment."[28] Under this prohibitor, people who have a conviction record for having been convicted of a misdemeanor crime of domestic violence (MCDV) under federal, state, or tribal law, that involved physical force or a threat with a deadly weapon, are prohibited from possessing or purchasing a firearm or ammunition.[29] Congress created this additional prohibitor in recognition of the reality that domestic abusers who committed felony violence were regularly pleading guilty to a misdemeanor crime[30] in order to avoid a trial that might result in a felony conviction. The Supreme Court subsequently interpreted the Lautenberg Amendment to be applied wherever someone was convicted of misdemeanor violence against an intimate partner, it did not matter whether or not the crime was called "domestic violence" in the law of the jurisdiction.[31] The MCDV prohibitor is the only prohibitor without an official use exemption for persons needing weapons to fulfill their duty while employed by a government agency.[32]

Both of these prohibitors are subject to a number of restrictions. First, they only apply to certain relationships. Both the DVPO prohibitor and the MCDV prohibitor apply when the abuser and the victim are current or former spouses, current or former cohabitants, are similarly situated as spouses, share a child in common, or the victim is the perpetrator's child.[33] The DVPO prohibitor also applies if the protective order protects the child of the intimate partner[34]; the MCDV prohibitor also applies to persons similarly situated to a spouse, parent, or guardian of the victim.[35]

Additionally, contrary to the claims of those who prioritize abusers' access to firearms over the lives of victims, both prohibitors protect the due process rights of the prohibited person. The Supreme Court has considered the MCDV prohibitor in three separate cases and has not raised any due process concerns.[36] Due process is written directly into the federal statute.[37]

Moreover, a DVPO lasts for a limited time. Although there are exceptions in state law for repeat offenders, most final DVPOs last between six months and two years, depending on the state or tribe issuing the protective order. At the expiration of the DVPO, that particular order ceases to trigger the federal firearms ban. In the case of an MCDV prohibitor, federal law stipulates that it does not apply to persons who have had their convictions expunged or set aside, have had their civil rights restored, or have been pardoned, unless the expungement, restoration, or pardon specifically says that they are still prohibited from possessing firearms.[38] Most misdemeanants who do not reoffend are eligible under state law to have their records expunged or to otherwise have their firearm access restored.

GAPS IN FEDERAL LAW

Federal law protects countless survivors from armed abusers, but it also fails to protect many others. For example, under federal law, dating partners are not prohibited from possessing firearms, nor are respondents to ex parte protective orders. Federal law likewise fails to protect survivors of stalking, whether by an intimate partner or not, by prohibiting adjudicated stalkers from possessing firearms. Furthermore, a technical fix to the MCDV prohibitor is necessary to ensure it applies uniformly nationwide. Solutions to these gaps will be explored in "Time to Bring Federal Domestic Violence Gun Laws in Line with Today's Reality" and "Local Laws and Local Enforcement Are Critical to Halt Gun Violence Between Intimate Partners" in the third part of this collection.

STATE LAW

In addition to the federal firearm prohibitors, states have also taken measures to disarm domestic abusers. In some cases, state laws mimic federal laws. In other states, they go beyond federal law, prohibiting current or former dating partners from possessing firearms, prohibiting respondents to ex parte protective orders (short-term, emergency orders issued after an initial hearing that only includes the petitioner) from possessing firearms, prohibiting adjudicated stalkers from possessing firearms, and requiring prohibited abusers to relinquish their firearms. Even in states without laws explicitly addressing abusers' access to firearms, judges issuing protective orders have general authority to remove firearms where such an order is crucial to the safety of the petitioner. For a state-by-state summary of domestic violence-related firearms laws, see disarmdv.org.

Strong state laws are important. Most domestic violence cases are handled at the state level, and state law enforcement agencies, prosecutors, and courts cannot enforce federal law. Local justice systems respond more quickly and consistently than federal systems to abusers who illegally possess firearms, so in many cases, it is better to implement state law prohibitions. Moreover, research shows that states that go beyond federal law to prohibit adjudicated dating abusers from possessing firearms have a 13 percent lower rate of intimate partner homicide.[39] States prohibiting respondents to ex parte protective orders as well as final protective orders also have a 13 percent lower rate of intimate partner homicides,[40] and states requiring prohibited abusers to relinquish their firearms have 12 percent lower rate of intimate partner homicide.[41]

GAP IN ENFORCEMENT

Enforcement is a key component to ensuring laws have their maximum impact. Unfortunately, research shows that enforcement is often severely lacking. Enforcement, to be successful, must include two important components: (1) making sure that people who are prohibited from possessing firearms do not acquire new ones; and (2) ensuring that persons prohibited by courts from possessing firearms relinquish firearms already in their possession.

> "[I worry about] the uncertainty of his thought process and his access to guns. Even though he couldn't have guns with the restraining order, he had them hidden in different places where he could have access to them." —Anonymous caller to the National Domestic Violence Hotline[42]

Federal law requires federally licensed firearms dealers to conduct background checks on all persons attempting to purchase firearms. Some states require background checks for all firearms transfers, not just for purchases from federally licensed dealers. Others require a permit to purchase firearms, and the background check is conducted at that time. The efficacy of the background check system is based on the quality and quantity of records submitted into the National Instant Criminal Background Check System and on its uniform use. In states where an abuser can legally evade completing a background check and in cases where disqualifying records have not been uploaded into the system or are incomplete, prohibited abusers can obtain firearms through legal means, even though it is illegal for them to possess those firearms.

Additionally, research shows that provisions in state law or in protective orders that require prohibited abusers to relinquish their firearms are rarely enforced. An exploratory study found that, in the sample, survivor reports indicated that only 12 percent of armed abusers prohibited from possessing firearms due to a protective order relinquished their firearms or had their firearms seized.[43] Enforcing firearms prohibitors and court orders are critical to protective survivors.

CONCLUSION

Armed abusers pose a risk to their victims, and their communities. Although both federal and state laws restricting abusers' access to firearms has significantly decreased intimate partner homicides, more must be done to keep guns out of the hands of domestic abusers. As will be explored in greater length in "Time to Bring Federal Domestic Violence Gun Laws in Line with Today's Reality" and "Local Laws and Local Enforcement Are Critical to Halt Gun Violence Between Intimate Partners," Congress and legislatures across the country can and should take action to protect survivors from armed abusers.

PART II

HOW WE GOT HERE

5

Battleground America
BY JILL LEPORE

Just after seven-thirty on the morning of February 27th, 2012, a seventeen-year-old boy named T. J. Lane walked into the cafeteria at Chardon High School, about thirty miles outside Cleveland. It was a Monday, and the cafeteria was filled with kids, some eating breakfast, some waiting for buses to drive them to programs at other schools, some packing up for gym class. Lane sat down at an empty table, reached into a bag, and pulled out a .22-calibre pistol. He stood up, raised the gun, and fired. He said not a word.

Russell King, a seventeen-year-old junior, was sitting at a table with another junior, Nate Mueller. King, shot in the head, fell face first onto the table, a pool of blood forming. A bullet grazed Mueller's ear. "I could see the flame at the end of the gun," Mueller said later. Daniel Parmertor, a sixteen-year-old snowboarder, was shot in the head. Someone screamed "Duck!" Demetrius Hewlin, sixteen, was also shot in the head, and slid under the table. Joy Rickers, a senior, tried to run; Lane shot her as she fled. Nickolas Walczak, shot in his neck, arm, back, and face, fell to the floor. He began crawling toward the door.

Ever since the shootings at Columbine High School, in a Denver suburb, in 1999, American schools have been preparing for gunmen. Chardon started holding drills in 2007, after the Virginia Tech massacre, when twenty-three-year-old Seung-Hui Cho, a college senior, shot fifty-seven people in Blacksburg.

At Chardon High School, kids ran through the halls screaming "Lockdown!" Some of them hid in the teachers' lounge; they barricaded the door with a piano. Someone got on the school's public-address system and gave instructions, but everyone knew what to do. Students ran into classrooms and dived under desks; teachers locked the doors and shut off the lights. Joseph Ricci, a math teacher, heard Walczak, who was still crawling, groaning in the hallway. Ricci opened the door and pulled the boy inside. No one knew if the shooter had more guns, or more rounds. Huddled under desks, students called 911 and texted their parents. One tapped out, "Prayforus."

From the cafeteria, Frank Hall, the assistant football coach, chased Lane out of the building, and he ran off into the woods.

Moments later, four ambulances arrived. E.M.T.s raced Rickers and Walczak to Chardon's Hillcrest Hospital. Hewlin, Parmertor, and King were flown by helicopter to a trauma center at MetroHealth Medical Center, in Cleveland. By eight-thirty, the high school had been evacuated.

At a quarter to nine, police officers with dogs captured Lane, about a mile from the school.

"I hate to say it, but we trained for exactly this type of thing, a school emergency of this type," Dan McClelland, the county sheriff, said.

Danny Parmertor died that afternoon. That evening, St. Mary's Church opened its doors, and the people of Chardon sank to their knees and keened. At the town square, students gathered to hold a vigil. As night fell, they lit candles. Drew Gittins, sixteen, played a Black Eyed Peas song on his guitar. "People killin', people dyin'," he sang. "People got me, got me questionin', Where is the love?"

Russell King had been too badly wounded. A little after midnight, doctors said that they couldn't save him.

■ ■ ■

There are nearly three hundred million privately owned firearms in the United States: a hundred and six million handguns, a hundred and five million rifles, and eighty-three million shotguns. That works out to about one gun for every American. The gun that T. J. Lane brought to Chardon High School belonged to his uncle, who had bought it in 2010, at a gun shop. Both of Lane's parents had been arrested on charges of domestic violence over the years. Lane found the gun in his grandfather's barn.

The United States is the country with the highest rate of civilian gun ownership in the world. (The second highest is Yemen, where the rate is nevertheless only half that of the U.S.) No civilian population is more powerfully armed. Most Americans do not, however, own guns, because three-quarters of people with guns own two or more. According to the General Social Survey, conducted by the National Policy Opinion Center at the University of Chicago, the prevalence of gun ownership has declined steadily in the past few decades. In 1973, there were guns in roughly one in two households in the United States; in 2010, one in three. In 1980, nearly one in three Americans owned a gun; in 2010, that figure had dropped to one in five.

Men are far more likely to own guns than women are, but the rate of gun ownership among men fell from one in two in 1980 to one in three in 2010, while, in that same stretch of time, the rate among women remained one in ten. What may have held that rate steady in an age of decline was the aggressive marketing of handguns to women for self-defense, which is how a great many guns are marketed. Gun ownership is higher among whites than among blacks, higher in the country than in the city, and higher among older people than among younger people. One reason that gun ownership is declining, nationwide, might be that high-school shooting clubs and rifle ranges at summer camps are no longer common.

Although rates of gun ownership, like rates of violent crime, are falling, the power of the gun lobby is not. Since 1980, forty-four states have passed some form of law that allows gun owners to carry concealed weapons outside their homes for personal protection. (Five additional states had these laws before 1980. Illinois is the sole holdout.) A federal ban on the possession, transfer, or manufacture of semiautomatic assault weapons, passed in 1994, was allowed to expire in 2004. In 2005, Florida passed the Stand Your Ground law, an extension of the so-called castle doctrine, exonerating from prosecution citizens who use deadly force when confronted by an assailant, even if they could have retreated safely; Stand Your Ground laws expand that protection outside the home to any place that an individual "has a right to be." Twenty-four states have passed similar laws.

The day before T. J. Lane shot five high-school students in Ohio, another high-school student was shot in Florida. The Orlando *Sentinel* ran a three-paragraph story. On February 26th, 2012, seventeen-year-old Trayvon Martin left a house in a town outside Orlando and walked to a store. He was seen by a twenty-eight-year-old man named George Zimmerman, who called 911 to report that Martin, who was black, was "a real suspicious guy." Zimmerman got out of his truck. Zimmerman was carrying a 9-mm. pistol; Martin was unarmed. What happened next has not been established, and is much disputed. Zimmerman told the police that Martin attacked him. Martin's family has said that the boy, heard over a cell phone, begged for his life.

Zimmerman shot Martin in the chest. Martin did not survive. Zimmerman was not charged. Outside Orlando, the story was not reported.

The day after the shooting in Ohio, I went to a firing range. I'd signed up for a lesson the week before. Once, when I was in Air Force R.O.T.C. for a year, I spent an afternoon studying how to defeat a sniper, but I'd never held a gun before.

The American Firearms School sits in an industrial park just north of Providence, in a beige stucco building topped with a roof of mint-green sheet metal. From the road, it looks like a bowling alley, but from the parking lot you can tell that it's not. You can hear the sound of gunfire. It doesn't sound like thunder. It doesn't sound like rain. It sounds like gunfire.

Inside, there's a shop, a pistol range, a rifle range, a couple of classrooms, a locker room, and a place to clean your gun. The walls are painted police blue up to the wainscoting, and then white to the ceiling, which is painted black. It feels like a clubhouse, except, if you've never been to a gun shop before, that part feels not quite licit, like a porn shop. On the floor, there are gun racks, gun cases, holsters, and gun safes. Rifles hang on a wall behind the counter; handguns are under glass. Most items, including the rifles, come in black or pink: there are pink handcuffs, a pink pistol grip, a pink gun case, and pink paper targets. Above the pink bull's-eye, which looks unnervingly like a breast, a line of text reads, "Cancer sucks."

The American Firearms School is run by Matt Medeiros, a Rhode Island firefighter and E.M.T. Medeiros is also a leader of the Rhode Island chapter of Pink Heals, a nonprofit organization of emergency and rescue workers who drive pink fire trucks and pink police cars to raise money for cancer research and support groups. Last year, when Pink Heals opened a women's center in West Warwick, Medeiros held a fund-raiser at the Firearms School.

Unlike many firing ranges, which are private clubs, the American Firearms School is open to the public. Most mornings, federal, state, and local law-enforcement agencies, as well as private security firms, rent out the ranges for training and target practice. Classes, from beginner to advanced, are held in the afternoons, and are run by certified instructors.

In many states, to purchase a gun from a licensed dealer you need a permit, which requires you to complete firearms-safety training, not unlike driver's education. But, even if all states required this, not everyone who buys a gun would have to take a class. That's because forty per cent of the guns purchased in the United States are bought from private sellers at gun shows, or through other private exchanges, such as classified ads, which fall under what is known as the "gun-show loophole" and are thus unregulated.

At the American Firearms School, the Learn to Shoot program, for novices, costs forty dollars for ninety minutes: a lesson, a gun rental, range time, two targets, and two boxes of bullets. This doesn't constitute sufficient instruction for a gun permit in the state, but the school offers a one-day, ninety-nine-dollar course that does: Basic Firearms Safety includes shooting fundamentals, a discussion of firearms law, and guidance in safe firearms storage.

The idea that every man can be his own policeman, and every woman hers, has necessitated revisions to the curriculum: civilians now receive training once available only to law-enforcement officers, or the military. A six-hour class on concealed carrying includes a lesson in "engaging the threat." N.R.A. Basic Personal Protection in the Home teaches "the basic knowledge, skills, and attitude essential to the safe and efficient use of a handgun for protection of self and family" and provides "information on the law-abiding individual's right to self-defense," while N.R.A. Basic Personal Protection Outside the Home is a two-day course. A primer lasting three hours provides "a tactical look at civilian life." This raises the question of just how much civilian life is left.

As I waited for my lesson, I paged through a stack of old magazines while watching Fox News on a flat-screen television. In Michigan and Arizona, Mitt Romney and Rick Santorum were competing in that day's Republican primaries. At the top of the hour came the headlines: in Ohio, Demetrius Hewlin had just died. For a tick, the news announcer fell silent.

I put down *Field and Stream* and picked up *American Rifleman*, a publication of the N.R.A. The magazine includes a regular column called "The Armed Citizen." A feature article introduced David Keene, the N.R.A.'s new president. Keene, who is sixty-six, is a longtime conservative political strategist. Grover Norquist once called him "a conservative Forrest Gump." The 2012 Presidential election, Keene told *American Rifleman*, is "perhaps the most crucial election, from a Second Amendment standpoint, in our lifetimes."

■ ■ ■

The Second Amendment reads, "A well-regulated militia being nec-essary to the security of a free State, the right of the people to keep and bear arms shall not be infringed." Arms are military weapons. A firearm is a cannon that you can carry, as opposed to artillery so big and heavy that you need wheels to move it, or people to help you. Cannons that you can carry around didn't exist until the Middle Ages. The first European firearms—essentially, tubes mounted on a pole—date to the end of the fourteenth century and are known as "hand cannons." Then came shoulder arms (that is, guns you can shoulder): muskets, rifles, and shotguns. A pistol is a gun that can be held in one hand. A revolver holds a number of bullets in a revolving chamber, but didn't become common until Samuel Colt patented his model in 1836. The firearms used by a well-regulated militia, at the time the Second Amendment was written, were mostly long arms that, like a smaller stockpile of pistols, could discharge only once before they had to be reloaded. In size, speed, efficiency, capacity, and sleekness, the differ-ence between an eighteenth-century musket and the gun that George Zimmerman was carrying is roughly the difference between the first laptop computer—which, not counting the external modem and the battery pack, weighed twenty-four pounds—and an iPhone.

A gun is a machine made to fire a missile that can bore through flesh. It can be used to hunt an animal or to commit or prevent a crime. Enough people carrying enough guns, and with the will and the training to use them, can defend a government, or topple one. For centuries before the first English colonists travelled to the New World, Parliament had been regulating the private ownership of fire-arms. (Generally, ownership was restricted to the wealthy; the prin-ciple was that anyone below the rank of gentleman found with a gun was a poacher.) England's 1689 Declaration of Rights made a provision that "subjects which are Protestants may have arms for their defence suitable to their condition and as allowed by law"; the Declaration was an attempt to resolve a struggle between Parliament and the Crown, in which Parliament wrested control of the militia from the Crown.

In the United States, Article VI of the Articles of Confederation, drafted in 1776 and ratified in 1781, required that "every state shall always keep up a well regulated and disciplined militia, sufficiently armed and accoutred, and shall provide and constantly have ready for use, in public stores, a due number of field pieces and tents, and a proper quantity of arms, ammunition and camp equipage." In early America, firearms and ammunition were often kept in public arsenals. In 1775, the British Army marched to Concord with the idea of seizing the arsenal where the Colonial militia stored its weapons. In January of 1787, a Massachusetts resident named Daniel Shays led eleven hundred men, many of them disaffected Revolutionary War veterans, in an attempt to capture an arsenal in Springfield; they had been protesting taxes, but they needed guns and ammunition. Springfield had been an arsenal since 1774. In 1777, George Washington, at the urging of Henry Knox, made it his chief northern arsenal. By 1786, Springfield housed the largest collection of weapons in the United States. In the winter of 1787, the governor of Massachusetts sent the militia to suppress the rebellion; the Springfield arsenal was defended. That spring, the Constitutional Convention met in Philadelphia. Among the matters the delegates were to take up was granting to the federal government the power to suppress insurgencies like Shays' Rebellion. From Boston, Benjamin Franklin's sister Jane wrote to him with some advice for "such a Number of wise men as you are connected with in the Convention": no more weapons, no more war. "I had Rather hear of the Swords being beat into Plow-shares, and the Halters used for Cart Roops, if by that means we may be brought to live Peaceably with won a nother."

The U.S. Constitution, which was signed in Philadelphia in September of 1787, granted Congress the power "to provide for calling forth the Militia to execute the Laws of the Union, suppress Insurrections and repel Invasions," the power "to provide for organizing, arming, and disciplining the Militia, and for governing such Part of them as may be employed in the Service of the United States, reserving to the States respectively, the Appointment of the Officers, and the Authority of training the Militia according to the discipline prescribed by Congress," and the power "to raise and support Armies, but no Appropriation of Money to that Use shall be for a longer Term than two Years."

Ratification was an uphill battle. The Bill of Rights, drafted by James Madison in 1789, offered assurance to Anti-Federalists, who feared that there would be no limit to the powers of the newly constituted federal government. Since one of their worries was the prospect of a standing army—a permanent army—Madison drafted an amendment guaranteeing the people the right to form a militia. In Madison's original version, the amendment read, "The right of the people to keep and bear arms shall not be infringed; a well armed and well regulated militia being the best security of a free country: but no person religiously scrupulous of bearing arms shall be compelled to render military service in person." This provision was made in the same spirit as the Third Amendment, which forbids the government to force you to have troops billeted in your home: "No Soldier shall, in time of peace be quartered in any house, without the consent of the Owner, nor in time of war, but in a manner to be prescribed by law."

None of this had anything to do with hunting. People who owned and used long arms to hunt continued to own and use them; the Second Amendment was not commonly understood as having any relevance to the shooting of animals. As Garry Wills once wrote, "One does not bear arms against a rabbit." Meanwhile, militias continued to muster—the Continental Army was disbanded at the end of the Revolutionary War—but the national defense was increasingly assumed by the United States Army; by the middle of the nineteenth century, the United States had a standing army, after all. Harpers Ferry was the U.S. Army's southern armory, Springfield its northern. In 1859, when John Brown and his men raided Harpers Ferry, they went there to get guns.

■ ■ ■

At the American Firearms School, you can either rent a gun or bring your own. It's like an ice-skating rink that way, except that renting skates when you don't know how to skate is different from renting a gun when you don't know how to shoot. The guys who work at the school don't take any chances. In the twelve years since the school opened, there has never been an accident. "You can't do anything here without us watching you," Tom Dietzel told me. "In a swimming pool, there are lifeguards. And this place is a lot more dangerous than a swimming pool."

Dietzel, who is twenty-four and has long dark hair, is one of the few instructors at the school who isn't ex-military, ex-police, or ex-rescue. He led me to a classroom, opened a case, and took out a .22-calibre Mark III Target Rimfire pistol. Dietzel studied history in college, and on weekends he gives tours of the Freedom Trail, in Boston. We talked about the eighteenth-century portraits in the new wing of the Museum of Fine Arts; we debated the oratory of Joseph Warren. Dietzel owns a flintlock musket; he's a Revolutionary War reënactor, with the Thirteenth Continental Regiment. He showed me a photograph of himself in costume: a cocked hat, a mustard-colored scarf of flax. He could have been painted by Gilbert Stuart.

Dietzel is a skilled and knowledgeable teacher, steady, patient, and calm. He had written safety rules on a whiteboard: Never point your gun at anyone. Keep your finger off the trigger. Don't trust the safety. Assume every gun is loaded.

He explained how to load the magazine. "This is a semiautomatic," he said. "After you fire, it will load the next bullet, but you have to pull the trigger again to fire. We don't have automatics here." Automatic weapons are largely banned by the federal government. "An automatic, you pull the trigger and it keeps shooting." Dietzel shook his head. "Because: why? Why?"

Gun owners may be more supportive of gun-safety regulations than is the leadership of the N.R.A. According to a 2009 Luntz poll, for instance, requiring mandatory background checks on all purchasers at gun shows is favored not only by eighty-five per cent of gun owners who are not members of the N.R.A. but also by sixty-nine per cent of gun owners who are.

Dietzel rose. "Stand like a shortstop about to field a ball," he said. He showed me how to hold the .22.

Every day, Dietzel goes to work and, at some point, has to hand a gun to a perfect stranger who has never used one. He went over the rules again.

We got earplugs and headgear and ammunition and went to the range. I fired a hundred rounds. Then Dietzel told me to go wash my hands, to get the gunpowder off, while he went to clean the gun.

The halls at the American Firearms School are decorated with framed prints: Monet's "Impression, Sunrise"; van Gogh's "Irises." A sign on the door of the women's restroom reads, "Every Tuesday Is Ladies Night. Ladies Get *FREE* Range Time from 5:00 PM to 9:00 PM."

I opened the door, and turned on the tap. T. J. Lane had used a .22-calibre Mark III Target Rimfire pistol. For a long time, I let the water run.

On March 8th, Trayvon Martin's father, Tracy Martin, held a press conference in Orlando. "We feel justice has not been served," he said. He demanded the release of recordings of calls to 911. "Family Wants Answers in Teen's Death," the Associated Press reported.

Two days later, the biggest gun show in New England was held in West Springfield, Massachusetts, in an exposition center the size of an airport hangar. (Nationwide, there are about five thousand gun shows annually.) Early in the morning, men with guns lined up to have them inspected at the door: two policemen made sure that every gun was unloaded; a plastic bucket on the floor, half filled with sand, was for dumping ammunition, like the bin at airport security where T.S.A. officers make you chuck your toothpaste. Tickets cost eleven dollars, but there was no charge for children younger than twelve.

Inside was a flea market: hundreds of folding tables draped with felt tablecloths and covered with guns, along with knives, swords, and a great deal of hunting gear. Long guns stood on their stocks, muzzles up. Handguns rested under glass, like jewelry. "Cash for Guns," the sign at the Tombstone Trading Company read. Ammunition was sold outdoors, in cartons, as in the fastener aisle of a hardware store. At the N.R.A. booth, membership came with a subscription to one of the N.R.A.'s three magazines, an N.R.A. baseball hat, twenty-five hundred dollars of insurance, "and the most important benefit of all—protecting the Constitution."

I stopped at the table of Guns, Inc., which advertises itself as the largest firearms dealer in western Massachusetts. Guns, Inc., is also an arsenal: a place where people who don't want to keep their guns at home can pay to have them stored.

In the nineteenth century, the Springfield Armory grew to become the single biggest supplier of long arms to the U.S. Army. It shut its doors in 1968. A National Historic Site now, it houses about ten thousand weapons, most of which are shoulder arms. A sign on the door warns that no firearms are allowed inside. "People ask about that," Richard Colton, a park ranger and the site's historian, told me when I visited, "but we have plenty of guns here already."

The story of the Springfield Armory illustrates a shift in the manufacture and storage of firearms: from public to private. In 1974, a family in Illinois founded a company devoted to arms manufacturing and import called Springfield Armory, Inc. The firm, "the first name in American firearms," is one of the largest of its kind in the United States. Dennis Reese, the current C.E.O., and his brother Tom have staunchly opposed gun regulation. I asked Brian Pranka, of Guns, Inc., if he had any Springfield Armory guns. He said, "You can't buy a Springfield handgun in Springfield." The company does not make handguns that conform to all the gun-safety regulations in states like Massachusetts, New York, and California, and in Illinois they have lobbied the legislature, successfully defeating a state ban on assault weapons. In 2008, the Illinois State Rifle Association gave the Reeses the Defenders of Freedom Award.

On the first day of the Springfield gun show, Trayvon Martin's parents appeared on "Good Morning America." On March 19th, the Department of Justice, responding to growing protests, announced that it would conduct an investigation. On March 23rd 2012, President Obama answered questions about the shooting at a press conference. "If I had a son, he'd look like Trayvon," the President said. Later that day, Rick Santorum spoke outside a firing range in West Monroe, Louisiana, where he'd just shot fourteen rounds from a Colt .45. He told the crowd, "What I was able to exercise was one of those fundamental freedoms that's guaranteed in our Constitution, the right to bear arms."

In the two centuries following the adoption of the Bill of Rights, in 1791, no amendment received less attention in the courts than the Second, except the Third. As Adam Winkler, a constitutional-law scholar at U.C.L.A., demonstrates in a remarkably nuanced new book, "Gunfight: The Battle Over the Right to Bear Arms in America," firearms have been regulated in the United States from the start. Laws banning the carrying of concealed weapons were passed in Kentucky and Louisiana in 1813, and other states soon followed: Indiana (1820), Tennessee and Virginia (1838), Alabama (1839), and Ohio (1859). Similar laws were passed in Texas, Florida, and Oklahoma. As the governor of Texas explained in 1893, the "mission of the concealed deadly weapon is murder. To check it is the duty of every self-respecting, law-abiding man."

Although these laws were occasionally challenged, they were rarely struck down in state courts; the state's interest in regulating the manufacture, ownership, and storage of firearms was plain enough. Even the West was hardly wild. "Frontier towns handled guns the way a Boston restaurant today handles overcoats in winter," Winkler writes. "New arrivals were required to turn in their guns to authorities in exchange for something like a metal token." In Wichita, Kansas, in 1873, a sign read, "Leave Your Revolvers at Police Headquarters, and Get a Check." The first thing the government of Dodge did when founding the city, in 1873, was pass a resolution that "any person or persons found carrying concealed weapons in the city of Dodge or violating the laws of the State shall be dealt with according to law." On the road through town, a wooden billboard read, "The Carrying of Firearms Strictly Prohibited." The shoot-out at the O.K. Corral, in Tombstone, Arizona, Winkler explains, had to do with a gun-control law. In 1880, Tombstone's city council passed an ordinance "to Provide against the Carrying of Deadly Weapons." When Wyatt Earp confronted Tom McLaury on the streets of Tombstone, it was because McLaury had violated that ordinance by failing to leave his gun at the sheriff's office.

The National Rifle Association was founded in 1871 by two men, a lawyer and a former reporter from the *New York Times*. For most of its history, the N.R.A. was chiefly a sporting and hunting association. To the extent that the N.R.A. had a political arm, it opposed some gun-control measures and supported many others, lobbying for new state laws in the nineteen-twenties and thirties, which introduced waiting periods for handgun buyers and required permits for anyone wishing to carry a concealed weapon. It also supported the 1934 National Firearms Act—the first major federal gun-control legislation—and the 1938 Federal Firearms Act, which together created a licensing system for dealers and prohibitively taxed the private ownership of automatic weapons ("machine guns"). The constitutionality of the 1934 act was upheld by the U.S. Supreme Court in 1939, in U.S. v. Miller, in which Franklin Delano Roosevelt's solicitor general, Robert H. Jackson, argued that the Second Amendment is "restricted to the keeping and bearing of arms by the people collectively for their common defense and security." Furthermore, Jackson said, the language of the amendment makes clear that the right "is not one which may be utilized for private purposes but only one which exists where the arms are borne in the militia or some other military organization provided for by law and intended for the protection of the state." The Court agreed, unanimously. In 1957, when the N.R.A. moved into new headquarters, its motto, at the building's entrance, read, "Firearms Safety Education, Marksmanship Training, Shooting for Recreation." It didn't say anything about freedom, or self-defense, or rights.

■ ■ ■

The modern gun debate began with a shooting. In 1963, Lee Harvey Oswald bought a bolt-action rifle—an Italian military-surplus weapon—for nineteen dollars and ninety-five cents by ordering it from an ad that he found in *American Rifleman*. Five days after Oswald assassinated President Kennedy, Thomas Dodd, a Democratic senator from Connecticut, introduced legislation restricting mail-order sales of shotguns and rifles. The N.R.A.'s executive vice-president, Franklin L. Orth, testified before Congress, "We do not think that any sane American, who calls himself an American, can object to placing into this bill the instrument which killed the president of the United States."

Gun-rights arguments have their origins not in eighteenth-century Anti-Federalism but in twentieth-century liberalism. They are the product of what the Harvard law professor Mark Tushnet has called the "rights revolution," the pursuit of rights, especially civil rights, through the courts. In the nineteen-sixties, gun ownership as a constitutional right was less the agenda of the N.R.A. than of black nationalists. In a 1964 speech, Malcolm X said, "Article number two of the constitutional amendments provides you and me the right to own a rifle or a shotgun." Establishing a constitutional right to carry a gun for the purpose of self-defense was part of the mission of the Black Panther Party for Self-Defense, which was founded in 1966. "Black People can develop Self-Defense Power by arming themselves from house to house, block to block, community to community throughout the nation," Huey Newton said.

In 1968, as Winkler relates, the assassinations of Robert Kennedy and Martin Luther King, Jr., gave the issue new urgency. A revised Gun Control Act banned mail-order sales, restricted the purchase of guns by certain high-risk people (e.g., those with criminal records), and prohibited the importation of military-surplus firearms. That law, along with a great deal of subsequent law-and-order legislation, was intended to fight crime, control riots, and solve what was called, in the age of the Moyni-

79

han report, the "Negro problem." The regulations that are part of these laws—firearms restrictions, mandatory-sentencing guidelines, abolition of parole, and the "war on drugs"—are now generally understood to be responsible for the dramatic rise in the U.S. incarceration rate.

The N.R.A. supported the 1968 Gun Control Act, with some qualms. Orth was quoted in *American Rifleman* as saying that although some elements of the legislation "appear unduly restrictive and unjustified in their application to law-abiding citizens, the measure as a whole appears to be one that the sportsmen of America can live with."

David Keene, the N.R.A.'s president, is the former chairman of the American Conservative Union. In his office in Washington, he has a photograph of Ronald Reagan on the wall and a view of Pennsylvania Avenue out the window. Keene has white hair, blue eyes, and an air of plainspoken geniality. When he was eight or nine, he says, his grandfather taught him how to shoot by aiming a .22 at squirrels and rabbits.

Keene's parents were labor organizers. They never once voted for a Republican. "My first political activity was going door to door passing out pamphlets for J.F.K. in the snows of Wisconsin," Keene told me. In the nineteen-fifties, he said, "Lionel Trilling considered conservatism to be a political pathology." Keene became a conservative in high school, when he read "The Constitution of Liberty," by Friedrich Hayek. In 1960, at the Republican National Convention, Barry Goldwater said, "Let's grow up conservatives, if we want to take this party back, and I think we can someday. Let's get to work." Four years later, Keene volunteered for Goldwater's campaign.

After Goldwater's defeat, Keene finished college and went on to law school. He became the national chairman of the Young Americans for Freedom. "What brought conservatism to dominance was the Great Society," Keene argues, because Johnson's vision represented "the culmination of the thinking that you could solve everything with money, and nothing worked." Keene went to D.C. to work for Spiro Agnew, and then for Richard Nixon.

On Election Day in 1970, Keene was at the White House. Joseph Tydings, a Democratic senator from Maryland who had introduced a Firearms Registration and Licensing Act, was running for reëlection. "The returns were coming in, and someone said, 'What's going on in Maryland?' " Keene recalled. "And someone answered, 'I can tell you this: everywhere except Baltimore, there are long lines of pickup trucks at the polls. He's going down over gun control.' "

In the nineteen-seventies, the N.R.A. began advancing the argument that the Second Amendment guarantees an individual's right to carry a gun, rather than the people's right to form armed militias to provide for the common defense. Fights over rights are effective at getting out the vote. Describing gun-safety legislation as an attack on a constitutional right gave conservatives a power at the polls that, at the time, the movement lacked. Opposing gun control was also consistent with a larger anti-regulation, libertarian, and anti-government conservative agenda. In 1975, the N.R.A. created a lobbying arm, the Institute for Legislative Action, headed by Harlon Bronson Carter, an award-winning marksman and a former chief of the U.S. Border Control. But then the N.R.A.'s leadership decided to back out of politics and move the organization's headquarters to Colorado Springs, where a new recreational-shooting facility was to be built. Eighty members of the N.R.A.'s staff, including Carter, were ousted. In 1977, the N.R.A.'s annual meeting, usually held in Washington, was moved to Cincinnati, in protest of the city's recent gun-control laws. Conservatives within the organization, led by Carter, staged what has come to be called the Cincinnati Revolt. The bylaws were rewritten and the old guard was pushed out. Instead of moving to Colorado, the N.R.A. stayed in D.C., where a new motto was displayed: "The Right of the People to Keep and Bear Arms Shall Not Be Infringed."

Ronald Reagan was the first Presidential candidate whom the N.R.A. had endorsed. David Keene ran Reagan's Southern campaign. Reagan's election, in 1980, made it possible for conservatives to begin turning a new interpretation of the Second Amendment into law. As the legal scholar Reva B. Siegel has chronicled, Orrin Hatch became the chair of the Subcommittee on the Constitution, and commissioned a history of the Second Amendment, which resulted in a 1982 report, "The Right to Keep and Bear Arms." The authors of the report claimed to have discovered "clear—and long-lost—proof that the Second Amendment to our Constitution was intended as an individual right of the American citizen to keep and carry arms in a peaceful manner, for protection of himself, his family, and his freedoms."

In March of 1981, John Hinckley, Jr., shot Reagan, the White House press secretary, James Brady, a D.C. policeman, and a Secret Service agent. He used a .22 that he had bought at a pawnshop. A month later, the *Times* reported that Harlon Carter, then the N.R.A.'s executive vice-president, had been convicted of murder in Laredo, Texas, in 1931, at the age of seventeen. Carter had come home from school to find his mother distressed. She told him that three teen-age boys had been loitering nearby all afternoon, and that she suspected them of having been involved in stealing the family's car. Carter left the house with a shotgun, found the boys, and told them that he wanted them to come back to his house to be questioned. According to the trial testimony of twelve-year-old Salvador Peña, Ramón Casiano, fifteen, the oldest of the boys, said to Carter, "We won't go to your house, and you can't make us." Casiano took out a knife and said, "Do you want to fight me?" Carter shot Casiano in the chest. At Carter's trial for murder, the judge, J. F. Mullally, instructed the jury, "There is no evidence that defendant had any lawful authority to require deceased to go to his house for questioning, and if defendant was trying to make deceased go there for that purpose at the time of the killing, he was acting without authority of law, and the law of self-defense does not apply." Two years later, Carter's murder conviction was overturned on appeal; the defense argued that the instructions to the jury had been improper.

When the *Times* broke the Casiano murder story, Carter at first denied it, saying the trial record concerned a different man with a similar name. He later said that he had "nothing to hide" and was "not going to rehash that case or any other that does not relate to the National Rifle Association."

James Brady and his wife, Sarah, went on to become active in the gun-control movement, but neither the assassination attempt nor Carter's past derailed the gun-rights movement. In 1986, the N.R.A.'s interpretation of the Second Amendment achieved new legal authority with the passage of the Firearms Owners Protection Act, which repealed parts of the 1968 Gun Control Act by invoking "the rights of citizens . . . to keep and bear arms under the Second Amendment." This interpretation was supported by a growing body of scholarship, much of it funded by the N.R.A. According to the constitutional-law scholar Carl Bogus, at least sixteen of the twenty-seven law-review articles published between 1970 and 1989 that were favorable to the N.R.A.'s interpretation of the Second Amendment were "written by lawyers who had been directly employed by or represented the N.R.A. or other gun-rights organizations." In an interview, former Chief Justice Warren Burger said that the new interpretation of the Second Amendment was "one of the greatest pieces of fraud, I repeat the word 'fraud,' on the American public by special-interest groups that I have ever seen in my lifetime."

The debate narrowed, and degraded. Political candidates who supported gun control faced opponents whose campaigns were funded by the N.R.A. In 1991, a poll found that Americans were more familiar with the Second Amendment than they were with the First: the right to speak and to believe, and to write and to publish, freely.

"If you had asked, in 1968, will we have the right to do with guns in 2012 what we can do now, no one, on either side, would have believed you," David Keene said.

Between 1968 and 2012, the idea that owning and carrying a gun is both a fundamental American freedom and an act of citizenship gained wide acceptance and, along with it, the principle that this right is absolute and cannot be compromised; gun-control legislation was diluted, defeated, overturned, or allowed to expire; the right to carry a concealed handgun became nearly ubiquitous; Stand Your Ground legislation passed in half the states; and, in 2008, in District of Columbia v. Heller, the Supreme Court ruled, in a 5–4 decision, that the District's 1975 Firearms Control Regulations Act was unconstitutional. Justice Scalia wrote, "The Second Amendment protects an individual right to possess a firearm unconnected with service in a militia." Two years later, in another 5–4 ruling, McDonald v. Chicago, the Court extended Heller to the states.

This issue has been delivering voters to the polls since 1970. Keene, in his lifetime, has witnessed a revolution. "It's not just the conservative political victories, the capture of the Republican Party, the creation of a conservative intellectual élite," he said, "but the whole change in the way Americans look at government." No conservative victories will last longer than the rulings of this Supreme Court.

One in three Americans knows someone who has been shot. As long as a candid discussion of guns is impossible, unfettered debate about the causes of violence is unimaginable. Gun-control advocates say the answer to gun violence is fewer guns. Gun-rights advocates say that the answer is more guns: things would have gone better, they suggest, if the faculty at Columbine, Virginia Tech, and Chardon High School had been armed. That is the logic of the concealed-carry movement; that is how armed citizens have come to be patrolling the streets. That is not how civilians live. When carrying a concealed weapon for self-defense is understood not as a failure of civil society, to be mourned, but as an act of citizenship, to be vaunted, there is little civilian life left.

In 2002, Keene's son David Michael Keene was driving on the George Washington Memorial Parkway when, in a road-rage incident, he fired a handgun at another motorist. He was sentenced to ten years in prison for "using, brandishing, and discharging a firearm in a crime of violence." I asked Keene if this private tragedy had left him uncertain about what the N.R.A. had wrought. He said no: "You break the law, you pay the price."

I asked Keene if any public atrocity had given him pause. He explained that it is the N.R.A.'s policy never to comment on a shooting.

I asked him how he would answer critics who charge that no single organization has done more to weaken Americans' faith in government, or in one another, than the N.R.A.

"We live in a society now that's Balkanized," Keene said. "But that has nothing to do with guns."

On Monday, March 26th 2012, thousands of students rallied in Atlanta, carrying signs that read, "I am Trayvon Martin," and "Don't Shoot!" One week later, in Oakland, a forty-three-year-old man named One Goh walked into Oikos University, a small Christian college. He was carrying a .45-calibre semiautomatic pistol and four magazines of ammunition. He grabbed Katleen Ping, a receptionist, and dragged her into a classroom. Nearby, Lucas Garcia, a thirty-three-year-old E.S.L. teacher, heard a voice call out, "Somebody's got a gun!" He helped his students escape through a back door. Dechen Yangdon, twenty-seven, turned off the lights in her classroom and locked the door. She could hear Ping screaming, "Help, help, help!" "We were locked inside," Yangdon said later. "We couldn't help her."

Goh ordered the students to line up against the wall. He said, "I'm going to kill you all."

They had come from all over the world. Ping, twenty-four, was born in the Philippines. She was working at the school to support her parents, her brother, two younger sisters, and her four-year-old son, Kayzzer. Her husband was hoping to move to the United States. Tshering Rinzing Bhutia, thirty-eight, was born in Gyalshing, India, in the foothills of the Himalayas. He took classes during the day; at night, he worked as a janitor at San Francisco International Airport. Lydia Sim, twenty-one, was born in San Francisco, to Korean parents; she wanted to become a pediatrician. Sonam Choedon, thirty-three, belonged to a family living in exile from Tibet. A Buddhist, she came to the United States from Dharamsala, India. She was studying to become a nurse. Grace Eunhea Kim, twenty-three, was putting herself through school by working as a waitress. Judith Seymour was fifty-three. Her parents had moved back to their native Guyana; her two children were grown. She was about to graduate. Doris Chibuko, forty, was born in Enugu, in eastern Nigeria, where she practiced law. She immigrated in 2002. Her husband, Efanye, works as a technician for A.T. & T. They had three children, ages eight, five, and three. She was two months short of completing a degree in nursing.

Ping, Bhutia, Sim, Choedon, Kim, Seymour, and Chibuko: Goh shot and killed them all. Then he went from one classroom to another, shooting, before stealing a car and driving away. He threw his gun into a tributary of San Leandro Bay. Shortly afterward, he walked into a grocery store and said, "I just shot some people."

On Tuesday night, a multilingual memorial service was held at the Allen Temple Baptist Church. Oakland's mayor, Jean Quan, said, "Oakland is a city of dreams." A friend of Choedon's said, "Mainly, we're praying for her next life, that she can have a better one." In Gyalshing, Bhutia's niece, Enchuk Namgyal, asked that her uncle's body be sent home to be cremated in the mountains above the village, across the world from the country where he came for an education, religious freedom, and economic opportunity, and was shot to death.

Kids in Chardon High are back in school. Nickolas Walczak is in a wheelchair. There are Trayvon Martin T-shirts. Oikos University is closed. The N.R.A. has no comment.

In an average year, roughly a hundred thousand Americans are killed or wounded with guns. On April 6th 2012, the police found One Goh's .45. Five days later, George Zimmerman was charged with second-degree murder. In May, T. J. Lane will appear at a hearing. Trials are to come. In each, introduced as evidence, will be an unloaded gun.

6

Dissent to District of Columbia v. Heller

BY JUSTICE JOHN PAUL STEVENS

In 2008, the Supreme Court returned a majority opinion on the case of District of Columbia, et al., petitioners v. Dick Anthony Heller *that ruled that the Second Amendment applied to the civilian possession of a weapon for "ordinary use," regardless of the relationship to a militia. This greatly expanded scope of Second Amendment and placed a new burden on federal gun legislation. The subsequent year, the same logic would be expanded to state regulation of firearms in* McDonald et al. v the City of Chicago, Illinois, et al.

The following are excerpts from Justice John Paul Stevens' dissenting opinion in Heller, *in which he was joined by Justices Souter, Ginsburg, and Breyer.*

To improve the reading experience for a lay audience, in-text citations in the following excerpts have been converted to endnotes.

The question presented by this case is not whether the Second Amendment protects a "collective right" or an "individual right." Surely it protects a right that can be enforced by individuals. But a conclusion that the Second Amendment protects an individual right does not tell us anything about the scope of that right.

Guns are used to hunt, for self-defense, to commit crimes, for sporting activities, and to perform military duties. The Second Amendment plainly does not protect the right to use a gun to rob a bank; it is equally clear that it *does* encompass the right to use weapons for certain military purposes. Whether it also protects the right to possess and use guns for nonmilitary purposes like hunting and personal self-defense is the question presented by this case. The text of the Amendment, its history, and our decision in *United States v. Miller*, 307 U. S. 174 (1939), provide a clear answer to that question.

The Second Amendment was adopted to protect the right of the people of each of the several States to maintain a well-regulated militia. It was a response to concerns raised during the ratification of the Constitution that the power of Congress to disarm the state militias and create a national standing army posed an intolerable threat to the sovereignty of the several States. Neither the text of the Amendment nor the arguments advanced by its proponents evidenced the slightest interest in limiting any legislature's authority to regulate private civilian uses of firearms. Specifically, there is no indication that the Framers of the Amendment intended to enshrine the common-law right of self-defense in the Constitution.

In 1934, Congress enacted the National Firearms Act, the first major federal firearms law. Upholding a conviction under that Act, this Court held that, "[i]n the absence of any evidence tending to show that possession or use of a 'shotgun having a barrel of less than eighteen inches in length' at this time has some reasonable relationship to the preservation or efficiency of a well regulated militia, we cannot say that the Second Amendment guarantees the right to keep and bear such an instrument."[1] The view of the Amendment we took in *Miller*— that it protects the right to keep and bear arms for certain military purposes, but that it does not curtail the Legislature's power to regulate the nonmilitary use and ownership of weapons—is both the most natural reading of the Amendment's text and the interpretation most faithful to the history of its adoption.

Since our decision in *Miller,* hundreds of judges have relied on the view of the Amendment we endorsed there; we ourselves affirmed it in 1980.[2] No new evidence has surfaced since 1980 supporting the view that the Amendment was intended to curtail the power of Congress to regulate civilian use or misuse of weapons. Indeed, a review of the drafting history of the Amendment demonstrates that its Framers *rejected* proposals that would have broadened its coverage to include such uses.

The opinion the Court announces today fails to identify any new evidence supporting the view that the Amendment was intended to limit the power of Congress to regulate civilian uses of weapons. Unable to point to any such evidence, the Court stakes its holding on a strained and unpersuasive reading of the Amendment's text; significantly different provisions in the 1689 English Bill of Rights, and in various 19th-century State Constitutions; postenactment commentary that was available to the Court when it decided *Miller;* and, ultimately, a feeble attempt to distinguish *Miller* that places more emphasis on the Court's decisional process than on the reasoning in the opinion itself.

Even if the textual and historical arguments on both sides of the issue were evenly balanced, respect for the well-settled views of all of our predecessors on this Court, and for the rule of law itself[3] would prevent most jurists from endorsing such a dramatic upheaval in the law. As Justice Cardozo observed years ago, the "labor of judges would be increased almost to the breaking point if every past decision could be reopened in every case, and one could not lay one's own course of bricks on the secure foundation of the courses laid by others who had gone before him."[4]

In this dissent I shall first explain why our decision in *Miller* was faithful to the text of the Second Amendment and the purposes revealed in its drafting history. I shall then comment on the postratification history of the Amendment, which makes abundantly clear that the Amendment should not be interpreted as limiting the authority of Congress to regulate the use or possession of firearms for purely civilian purposes.

I

The text of the Second Amendment is brief. It provides: "A well regulated Militia, being necessary to the security of a free State, the right of the people to keep and bear Arms, shall not be infringed."

Three portions of that text merit special focus: the introductory language defining the Amendment's purpose, the class of persons encompassed within its reach, and the unitary nature of the right that it protects.

"A well regulated Militia, being necessary to the security of a free State"

The preamble to the Second Amendment makes three important points. It identifies the preservation of the militia as the Amendment's purpose; it explains that the militia is necessary to the security of a free State; and it recognizes that the militia must be "well regulated." In all three respects it is comparable to provisions in several State Declarations of Rights that were adopted roughly contemporaneously with the Declaration of Independence. Those state provisions highlight the importance members of the founding generation attached to the maintenance of state militias; they also underscore the profound fear shared by many in that era of the dangers posed by standing armies. While the need for state militias has not been a matter of significant public interest for almost two centuries, that fact should not obscure the contemporary concerns that animated the Framers.

The parallels between the Second Amendment and these state declarations, and the Second Amendment's omission of any statement of purpose related to the right to use firearms for hunting or personal self-defense, is especially striking in light of the fact that the Declarations of Rights of Pennsylvania and Vermont *did* expressly protect such civilian uses at the time. Article XIII of Pennsylvania's 1776 Declaration of Rights announced that "the people have a right to bear arms for the defence *of themselves* and the state,"[5] (emphasis added); [section] 43 of the Declaration assured that "the inhabitants of this state shall have the liberty to fowl and hunt in seasonable times on the lands they hold, and on all other lands therein not inclosed,"[6]. And Article XV of the 1777 Vermont Declaration of Rights guaranteed "[t]hat the people have a right to bear arms for the defence *of themselves* and the State."[7] (emphasis added). The contrast between those two declarations and the Second Amendment reinforces the clear statement of purpose announced in the Amendment's preamble. It confirms that the Framers' single-minded focus in crafting the constitutional guarantee "to keep and bear arms" was on military uses of firearms, which they viewed in the context of service in state militias.

The preamble thus both sets forth the object of the Amendment and informs the meaning of the remainder of its text. Such text should not be treated as mere surplusage, for "[i]t cannot be presumed that any clause in the constitution is intended to be without effect."[8]

The Court today tries to denigrate the importance of this clause of the Amendment by beginning its analysis with the Amendment's operative provision and returning to the preamble merely "to ensure that our reading of the operative clause is consistent with the announced purpose."[9] That is not how this Court ordinarily reads such texts, and it is not how the preamble would have been viewed at the time the Amendment was adopted. While the Court makes the novel suggestion that it need only find some "logical connection" between the preamble and the operative provision, it does acknowledge that a prefatory clause may resolve an ambiguity in the text.[10] Without identifying any language in the text that even mentions civilian uses of firearms, the Court proceeds to "find" its preferred reading in what is at best an ambiguous text, and then concludes that its reading is not foreclosed by the preamble. Perhaps the Court's approach to the text is acceptable advocacy, but it is surely an unusual approach for judges to follow.

"The right of the people"

The centerpiece of the Court's textual argument is its insistence that the words "the people" as used in the Second Amendment must have the same meaning, and protect the same class of individuals, as when they are used in the First and Fourth Amendments. According to the Court, in all three provisions—as well as the Constitution's preamble, section 2 of Article I, and the Tenth Amendment—"the term unambiguously refers to all members of the political community, not an unspecified subset."[11] But the Court *itself* reads the Second Amendment to protect a "subset" significantly narrower than the class of persons protected by the First and Fourth Amendments; when it finally drills down on the substantive meaning of the Second Amendment, the Court limits the protected class to "law-abiding, responsible citizens[.]"[12] But the class of persons protected by the First and Fourth Amendments is *not* so limited; for even felons (and presumably irresponsible citizens as well) may invoke the protections of those constitutional provisions. The Court offers no way to harmonize its conflicting pronouncements.

The Court also overlooks the significance of the way the Framers used the phrase "the people" in these constitutional provisions. In the First Amendment, no words define the class of individuals entitled to speak, to publish, or to worship; in that Amendment it is only the right peaceably to assemble, and to petition the Government for a redress of grievances, that is described as a right of "the people." These rights contemplate collective action. While the right peaceably to assemble protects the individual rights of those persons participating in the assembly, its concern is with action engaged in by members of a group, rather than any single individual. Likewise, although the act of petitioning the Government is a right that can be exercised by individuals, it is primarily collective in nature. For if they are to be effective, petitions must involve groups of individuals acting in concert.

Similarly, the words "the people" in the Second Amendment refer back to the object announced in the Amendment's preamble. They remind us that it is the collective action of individuals having a duty to serve in the militia that the text directly protects and, perhaps more importantly, that the ultimate purpose of the Amendment was to protect the States' share of the divided sovereignty created by the Constitution.

As used in the Fourth Amendment, "the people" describes the class of persons protected from unreasonable searches and seizures by Government officials. It is true that the Fourth Amendment describes a right that need not be exercised in any collective sense. But that observation does not settle the meaning of the phrase "the people" when used in the Second Amendment. For, as we have seen, the phrase means something quite different in the Petition and Assembly Clauses of the First Amendment. Although the abstract definition of the phrase "the people" could carry the same meaning in the Second Amendment as in the Fourth Amendment, the preamble of the Second Amendment suggests that the uses of the phrase in the First and Second Amendments are the same in referring to a collective activity. By way of contrast, the Fourth Amendment describes a right *against* governmental interference rather than an affirmative right *to* engage in protected conduct, and so refers to a right to protect a purely individual interest. As used in the Second Amendment, the words "the people" do not enlarge the right to keep and bear arms to encompass use or ownership of weapons outside the context of service in a well-regulated militia.

"To keep and bear Arms"

Although the Court's discussion of these words treats them as two "phrases"—as if they read "to keep" and "to bear"—they describe a unitary right: to possess arms if needed for military purposes and to use them in conjunction with military activities.

As a threshold matter, it is worth pausing to note an oddity in the Court's interpretation of "to keep and bear arms." Unlike the Court of Appeals, the Court does not read that phrase to create a right to possess arms for "lawful, private purposes."[13] Instead, the Court limits the Amendment's protection to the right "to possess and carry weapons in case of confrontation."[14] No party or *amicus* urged this interpretation; the Court appears to have fashioned it out of whole cloth. But although this novel limitation lacks support in the text of the Amendment, the Amendment's text *does* justify a different limitation: the "right to keep and bear arms" protects only a right to possess and use firearms in connection with service in a state-organized militia.

The term "bear arms" is a familiar idiom; when used unadorned by any additional words, its meaning is "to serve as a soldier, do military service, fight."[15] It is derived from the Latin *arma ferre,* which, translated literally, means "to bear *[ferre]* war equipment *[arma].*"[16] One 18th-century dictionary defined "arms" as "weapons of offence, or armour of defence,"[17], and another contemporaneous source explained that "[b]y *arms,* we understand those instruments of offence generally made use of in war; such as firearms, swords, & c. By *weapons,* we more particularly mean instruments of other kinds (exclusive of fire-arms), made use of as offensive, on special occasions."[18] Had the Framers wished to expand the meaning of the phrase "bear arms" to encompass civilian possession and use, they could have done so by the addition of phrases such as "for the defense of themselves," as was done in the Pennsylvania and Vermont Declarations of Rights. The *unmodified* use of "bear arms," by contrast, refers most naturally to a military purpose, as evidenced by its use in literally dozens of contemporary texts. The absence of any reference to civilian uses of weapons tailors the text of the Amendment to the purpose identified in its preamble. But when discussing these words, the Court simply ignores the preamble.

The Court argues that a "qualifying phrase that contradicts the word or phrase it modifies is unknown this side of the looking glass."[19] But this fundamentally fails to grasp the point. The stand-alone phrase "bear arms" most naturally conveys a military meaning *unless* the addition of a qualifying phrase signals that a different meaning is intended. When, as in this case, there is no such qualifier, the most natural meaning is the military one; and, in the absence of any qualifier, it is all the more appropriate to look to the preamble to confirm the natural meaning of the text. The Court's objection is particularly puzzling in light of its own contention that the addition of the modifier "against" changes the meaning of "bear arms." Compare [the opinion of the Court in *District of Columbia v. Heller*], at [page] 10 (defining "bear arms" to mean "carrying [a weapon] for a particular purpose—confrontation"), with [the opinion of the Court], at [page] 12 ("The phrase 'bear Arms' also had at the time of the founding an idiomatic meaning that was significantly different from its natural meaning: to serve as a soldier, do military service, fight or to wage war. But it unequivocally bore that idiomatic meaning only when followed by the preposition 'against.'" (citations and some internal quotation marks omitted)).

The Amendment's use of the term "keep" in no way contradicts the military meaning conveyed by the phrase "bear arms" and the Amendment's preamble. To the contrary, a number of state militia laws in effect at the time of the Second Amendment's drafting used the term "keep" to describe the requirement that militia members store their arms at their homes, ready to be used for service when necessary. The Virginia military law, for example, ordered that "every one of the said officers, non-commissioned officers, and privates, shall constantly *keep* the aforesaid arms, accoutrements, and ammunition, ready to be produced whenever called for by his commanding officer."[20] (emphasis added). "[K]eep and bear arms" thus perfectly describes the responsibilities of a framing-era militia member.

This reading is confirmed by the fact that the clause protects only one right, rather than two. It does not describe a right "to keep arms" and a separate right "to bear arms." Rather, the single right that it does describe is both a duty and a right to have arms available and ready for military service, and to use them for military purposes when necessary. Different language surely would have been used to protect nonmilitary use and possession of weapons from regulation if such an intent had played any role in the drafting of the Amendment.

When each word in the text is given full effect, the Amendment is most naturally read to secure to the people a right to use and possess arms in conjunction with service in a well-regulated militia. So far as appears, no more than that was contemplated by its drafters or is encompassed within its terms. Even if the meaning of the text were genuinely susceptible to more than one interpretation, the burden would remain on those advocating a departure from the purpose identified in the preamble and from settled law to come forward with persuasive new arguments or evidence. The textual analysis offered by respondent and embraced by the Court falls far short of sustaining that heavy burden. And the Court's emphatic reliance on the claim "that the Second Amendment . . . codified a *pre-existing* right,"[21] is of course beside the point because the right to keep and bear arms for service in a state militia was also a pre-existing right.

Indeed, not a word in the constitutional text even arguably supports the Court's overwrought and novel description of the Second Amendment as "elevat[ing] above all other interests" "the right of law-abiding, responsible citizens to use arms in defense of hearth and home."[22]

II

The proper allocation of military power in the new Nation was an issue of central concern for the Framers. The compromises they ultimately reached, reflected in Article I's Militia Clauses and the Second Amendment, represent quintessential examples of the Framers' "splitting the atom of sovereignty."

Two themes relevant to our current interpretive task ran through the debates on the original Constitution. "On the one hand, there was a widespread fear that a national standing Army posed an intolerable threat to individual liberty and to the sovereignty of the separate States."[23] Governor Edmund Randolph, reporting on the Constitutional Convention to the Virginia Ratification Convention, explained: "With respect to a standing army, I believe there was not a member in the federal Convention, who did not feel indignation at such an institution."[24] On the other hand, the Framers recognized the dangers inherent in relying on inadequately trained militia members "as the primary means of providing for the common defense,"[25]; during the Revolutionary War, "[t]his force, though armed, was largely untrained, and its deficiencies were the subject of bitter complaint."[26] In order to respond to those twin concerns, a compromise was reached: Congress would be authorized to raise and support a national Army and Navy, and also to organize, arm, discipline, and provide for the calling forth of "the Militia."[27] The President, at the same time, was empowered as the "Commander in Chief of the Army and Navy of the United States, and of the Militia of the several States, when called into the actual Service of the United States."[28] But, with respect to the militia, a significant reservation was made to the States: Although Congress would have the power to call forth, organize, arm, and discipline the militia, as well as to govern "such Part of them as may be employed in the Service of the United States," the States respectively would retain the right to appoint the officers and to train the militia in accordance with the discipline prescribed by Congress.[29]

But the original Constitution's retention of the militia and its creation of divided authority over that body did not prove sufficient to allay fears about the dangers posed by a standing army. For it was perceived by some that Article I contained a significant gap: While it empowered Congress to organize, arm, and discipline the militia, it did not prevent Congress from providing for the militia's *dis*armament. As George Mason argued during the debates in Virginia on the ratification of the original Constitution:

"The militia may be here destroyed by that method which has been practiced in other parts of the world before; that is, by rendering them useless—by disarming them. Under various pretences, Congress may neglect to provide for arming and disciplining the militia; and the state governments cannot do it, for Congress has the exclusive right to arm them."[30]

This sentiment was echoed at a number of state ratification conventions; indeed, it was one of the primary objections to the original Constitution voiced by its opponents. The Anti-Federalists were ultimately unsuccessful in persuading state ratification conventions to condition their approval of the Constitution upon the eventual inclusion of any particular amendment. But a number of States did propose to the first Federal Congress amendments reflecting a desire to ensure that the institution of the militia would remain protected under the new Government. The proposed amendments sent by the States of Virginia, North Carolina, and New York focused on the importance of preserving the state militias and reiterated the dangers posed by standing armies. New Hampshire sent a proposal that differed significantly from the others; while also invoking the dangers of a standing army, it suggested that the Constitution should more broadly protect the use and possession of weapons, without tying such a guarantee expressly to the maintenance of the militia. The States of Maryland, Pennsylvania, and Massachusetts sent no relevant proposed amendments to Congress, but in each of those States a minority of the delegates advocated related amendments. While the Maryland minority proposals were exclusively concerned with standing armies and conscientious objectors, the unsuccessful proposals in both Massachusetts and Pennsylvania would have protected a more broadly worded right, less clearly tied to service in a state militia. Faced with all of these options, it is telling that James Madison chose to craft the Second Amendment as he did.

The relevant proposals sent by the Virginia Ratifying Convention read as follows:

> "17th. That the people have a right to keep and bear
> arms; that a well regulated Militia composed of the
> body of the people trained to arms is the proper,

natural and safe defence of a free State. That standing armies are dangerous to liberty, and therefore ought to be avoided, as far as the circumstances and protection of the Community will admit; and that in all cases the military should be under strict subordination to and be governed by the civil power."[31]

"19th. That any person religiously scrupulous of bearing arms ought to be exempted, upon payment of an equivalent to employ another to bear arms in his stead."[32]

North Carolina adopted Virginia's proposals and sent them to Congress as its own, although it did not actually ratify the original Constitution until Congress had sent the proposed Bill of Rights to the States for ratification.[33]

New York produced a proposal with nearly identical language. It read:

"That the people have a right to keep and bear Arms; that a well regulated Militia, including the body of the People capable of bearing Arms, is the proper, natural, and safe defence of a free State . . . That standing Armies, in time of Peace, are dangerous to Liberty, and ought not to be kept up, except in Cases of necessity; and that at all times, the Military should be kept under strict Subordination to the civil Power."[34]

Notably, each of these proposals used the phrase "keep and bear arms," which was eventually adopted by Madison. And each proposal embedded the phrase within a group of principles that are distinctly military in meaning.

By contrast, New Hampshire's proposal, although it followed another proposed amendment that echoed the familiar concern about standing armies, described the protection involved in more clearly personal terms. Its proposal read:

> *"Twelfth,* Congress shall never disarm any Citizen unless such as are or have been in Actual Rebellion."[35]

The proposals considered in the other three States, although ultimately rejected by their respective ratification conventions, are also relevant to our historical inquiry. First, the Maryland proposal, endorsed by a minority of the delegates and later circulated in pamphlet form, read:

> "4 .That no standing army shall be kept up in time of peace, unless with the consent of two thirds of the members present of each branch of Congress.
>
>   . . .
>
> "10. That no person conscientiously scrupulous of bearing arms in any case, shall be compelled personally to serve as a soldier."[36]

The rejected Pennsylvania proposal, which was later incorporated into a critique of the Constitution titled "The Address and Reasons of Dissent of the Pennsylvania Minority of the Convention of the State of Pennsylvania to Their Constituents (1787)," signed by a minority of the State's delegates (those who had voted against ratification of the Constitution),[37] read:

> "7. That the people have a right to bear arms for the defense of themselves and their own State, or the

> United States, or for the purpose of killing game;
> and no law shall be passed for disarming the people
> or any of them unless for crimes committed, or real
> danger of public injury from individuals; and as
> standing armies in the time of peace are dangerous
> to liberty, they ought not to be kept up; and that the
> military shall be kept under strict subordination to,
> and be governed by the civil powers."[38]

Finally, after the delegates at the Massachusetts Ratification Convention had compiled a list of proposed amendments and alterations, a motion was made to add to the list the following language: "[T]hat the said Constitution never be construed to authorize Congress to . . . prevent the people of the United States, who are peaceable citizens, from keeping their own arms."[39] This motion, however, failed to achieve the necessary support, and the proposal was excluded from the list of amendments the State sent to Congress.[40]

Madison, charged with the task of assembling the proposals for amendments sent by the ratifying States, was the principal draftsman of the Second Amendment. He had before him, or at the very least would have been aware of, all of these proposed formulations. In addition, Madison had been a member, some years earlier, of the committee tasked with drafting the Virginia Declaration of Rights. That committee considered a proposal by Thomas Jefferson that would have included within the Virginia Declaration the following language: "No freeman shall ever be debarred the use of arms [within his own lands or tenements]."[41] But the committee rejected that language, adopting instead the provision drafted by George Mason.

> With all of these sources upon which to draw, it
> is strikingly significant that Madison's first draft
> omitted any mention of nonmilitary use or posses-
> sion of weapons. Rather, his original draft repeated
> the essence of the two proposed amendments sent

by Virginia, combining the substance of the two
provisions succinctly into one, which read: "The
right of the people to keep and bear arms shall not
be infringed; a well armed, and well regulated militia being the best security of a free country; but no
person religiously scrupulous of bearing arms, shall
be compelled to render military service in person."[42]

Madison's decision to model the Second Amendment on the distinctly military Virginia proposal is therefore revealing, since it is
clear that he considered and rejected formulations that would have
unambiguously protected civilian uses of firearms. When Madison
prepared his first draft, and when that draft was debated and modified,
it is reasonable to assume that all participants in the drafting process
were fully aware of the other formulations that would have protected
civilian use and possession of weapons and that their choice to craft
the Amendment as they did represented a rejection of those alternative formulations.

Madison's initial inclusion of an exemption for conscientious objectors sheds revelatory light on the purpose of the Amendment. It
confirms an intent to describe a duty as well as a right, and it unequivocally identifies the military character of both. The objections
voiced to the conscientious-objector clause only confirm the central
meaning of the text. Although records of the debate in the Senate,
which is where the conscientious-objector clause was removed, do
not survive, the arguments raised in the House illuminate the perceived problems with the clause: Specifically, there was concern
that Congress "can declare who are those religiously scrupulous,
and prevent them from bearing arms." The ultimate removal of the
clause, therefore, only serves to confirm the purpose of the Amendment—to protect against congressional disarmament, by whatever
means, of the States' militias.

The Court also contends that because "Quakers opposed the use
of arms not just for militia service, but for any violent purpose what-
soever,"[43] the inclusion of a conscientious-objector clause in the origi-

nal draft of the Amendment does not support the conclusion that the phrase "bear arms" was military in meaning. But that claim cannot be squared with the record. In the proposals cited *supra,* at [pp. 100-102], both Virginia and North Carolina included the following language: "That any person religiously scrupulous of bearing arms ought to be exempted, upon payment of an equivalent *to employ another to bear arms in his stead"* (emphasis added). There is no plausible argument that the use of "bear arms" in those provisions was not unequivocally and exclusively military: The State simply does not compel its citizens to carry arms for the purpose of private "confrontation,"[44] or for self-defense.

The history of the adoption of the Amendment thus describes an overriding concern about the potential threat to state sovereignty that a federal standing army would pose, and a desire to protect the States' militias as the means by which to guard against that danger. But state militias could not effectively check the prospect of a federal standing army so long as Congress retained the power to disarm them, and so a guarantee against such disarmament was needed. As we explained in *Miller:* "With obvious purpose to assure the continuation and render possible the effectiveness of such forces the declaration and guarantee of the Second Amendment were made. It must be interpreted and applied with that end in view."[45] The evidence plainly refutes the claim that the Amendment was motivated by the Framers' fears that Congress might act to regulate any civilian uses of weapons. And even if the historical record were genuinely ambiguous, the burden would remain on the parties advocating a change in the law to introduce facts or arguments "'newly ascertained,'"[46]; the Court is unable to identify any such facts or arguments.

[. . .]

The brilliance of the debates that resulted in the Second Amendment faded into oblivion during the ensuing years, for the concerns about Article I's Militia Clauses that generated such pitched debate during the ratification process and led to the adoption of the Second Amendment were short lived.

In 1792, the year after the Amendment was ratified, Congress passed a statute that purported to establish "an Uniform Militia throughout the United States."[47] The statute commanded every able-bodied white male citizen between the ages of 18 and 45 to be enrolled therein and to "provide himself with a good musket or fire-lock" and other specified weaponry.[48] The statute is significant, for it confirmed the way those in the founding generation viewed fire-arm ownership: as a duty linked to military service. The statute they enacted, however, "was virtually ignored for more than a century," and was finally repealed in 1901.[49]

The postratification history of the Second Amendment is strikingly similar. The Amendment played little role in any legislative debate about the civilian use of firearms for most of the 19th century, and it made few appearances in the decisions of this Court. Two 19th-century cases, however, bear mentioning.

In *United States* v. *Cruikshank*, 92 U. S. 542 (1876), the Court sustained a challenge to respondents' convictions under the Enforcement Act of 1870 for conspiring to deprive any individual of "'any right or privilege granted or secured to him by the constitution or laws of the United States.'"[50] The Court wrote, as to counts 2 and 10 of respondents' indictment:

> "The right there specified is that of 'bearing arms for a lawful purpose.' This is not a right granted by the Constitution. Neither is it in any manner dependent on that instrument for its existence. The second amendment declares that it shall not be infringed; but this, as has been seen, means no more than that it shall not be infringed by Congress. This is one of the amendments that has no other effect than to restrict the powers of the national government."[51]

The majority's assertion that the Court in *Cruikshank* "described the right protected by the Second Amendment as '"bearing arms for a lawful purpose,"""[52], is not accurate. The *Cruikshank* Court explained that the defective *indictment* contained such language, but the Court did not itself describe the right, or endorse the indictment's description of the right.

Moreover, it is entirely possible that the basis for the indictment's counts 2 and 10, which charged respondents with depriving the victims of rights secured by the Second Amendment, was the prosecutor's belief that the victims—members of a group of citizens, mostly black but also white, who were rounded up by the Sheriff, sworn in as a posse to defend the local courthouse, and attacked by a white mob—bore sufficient resemblance to members of a state militia that they were brought within the reach of the Second Amendment.[53]

Only one other 19th-century case in this Court, *Presser* v. *Illinois*, 116 U. S. 252 (1886), engaged in any significant discussion of the Second Amendment. The petitioner in *Presser* was convicted of violating a state statute that prohibited organizations other than the Illinois National Guard from associating together as military companies or parading with arms. Presser challenged his conviction, asserting, as relevant, that the statute violated both the Second and the Fourteenth Amendments. With respect to the Second Amendment, the Court wrote:

> "We think it clear that the sections under consideration, which only forbid bodies of men to associate together as military organizations, or to drill or parade with arms in cities and towns unless authorized by law, do not infringe the right of the people to keep and bear arms. But a conclusive answer to the contention that this amendment prohibits the legislation in question lies in the fact that the amendment is a limitation only upon the power of Congress and the National government, and not upon that of the States."[54]

And in discussing the Fourteenth Amendment, the Court explained:

> "The plaintiff in error was not a member of the
> organized volunteer militia of the State of Illinois,
> nor did he belong to the troops of the United States
> or to any organization under the militia law of the
> United States. On the contrary, the fact that he did
> not belong to the organized militia or the troops of
> the United States was an ingredient in the offence
> for which he was convicted and sentenced. The
> question is, therefore, had he a right as a citizen of
> the United States, in disobedience of the State law,
> to associate with others as a military company, and
> to drill and parade with arms in the towns and cit-
> ies of the State? If the plaintiff in error has any such
> privilege he must be able to point to the provision
> of the Constitution or statutes of the United States
> by which it is conferred."[55]

Presser, therefore, both affirmed *Cruikshank's* holding that the Second Amendment posed no obstacle to regulation by state governments, and suggested that in any event nothing in the Constitution protected the use of arms outside the context of a militia "authorized by law" and organized by the State or Federal Government.

In 1901 the President revitalized the militia by creating "'the National Guard of the several States,'"[56]; meanwhile, the dominant understanding of the Second Amendment's inapplicability to private gun owner-ship continued well into the 20th century. The first two federal laws directly restricting civilian use and possession of firearms—the 1927 Act prohibiting mail delivery of "pistols, revolvers, and other firearms capable of being concealed on the person,"[57] and the 1934 Act prohib-iting the possession of sawed-off shotguns and machine guns—were enacted over minor Second Amendment objections dismissed by the vast majority of the legislators who participated in the debates. Members of Congress clashed over the wisdom and efficacy of such laws as crime-control measures. But since the statutes did not infringe upon the military use or possession of weapons, for most legislators they did not even raise the specter of possible conflict with the Second Amendment.

Thus, for most of our history, the invalidity of Second-Amendment-based objections to firearms regulations has been well settled and uncontroversial. Indeed, the Second Amendment was not even mentioned in either full House of Congress during the legislative proceedings that led to the passage of the 1934 Act. Yet enforcement of that law produced the judicial decision that confirmed the status of the Amendment as limited in reach to military usage. After reviewing many of the same sources that are discussed at greater length by the Court today, the *Miller* Court unanimously concluded that the Second Amendment did not apply to the possession of a firearm that did not have "some reasonable relationship to the preservation or efficiency of a well regulated militia."[58]

The key to that decision did not, as the Court belatedly suggests,[59] turn on the difference between muskets and sawed-off shotguns; it turned, rather, on the basic difference between the military and non-military use and possession of guns. Indeed, if the Second Amendment were not limited in its coverage to military uses of weapons, why should the Court in *Miller* have suggested that some weapons but not others were eligible for Second Amendment protection? If use for self-defense were the relevant standard, why did the Court not inquire into the suitability of a particular weapon for self-defense purposes?

[. . .]

Until today, it has been understood that legislatures may regulate the civilian use and misuse of firearms so long as they do not interfere with the preservation of a well-regulated militia. The Court's announcement of a new constitutional right to own and use firearms for private purposes upsets that settled understanding, but leaves for future cases the formidable task of defining the scope of permissible regulations. Today judicial craftsmen have confidently asserted that a policy choice that denies a "law-abiding, responsible citize[n]" the right to keep and use weapons in the home for self-defense is "off the table."[60] Given the presumption that most citizens are law abiding, and the reality that the need to defend oneself may suddenly arise in a host of locations outside the home, I fear that the District's policy choice may well be just the first of an unknown number of dominoes to be knocked off the table.

I do not know whether today's decision will increase the labor of federal judges to the "breaking point" envisioned by Justice Cardozo, but it will surely give rise to a far more active judicial role in making vitally important national policy decisions than was envisioned at any time in the 18th, 19th, or 20th centuries.

The Court properly disclaims any interest in evaluating the wisdom of the specific policy choice challenged in this case, but it fails to pay heed to a far more important policy choice—the choice made by the Framers themselves. The Court would have us believe that over 200 years ago, the Framers made a choice to limit the tools available to elected officials wishing to regulate civilian uses of weapons, and to authorize this Court to use the common-law process of case-by-case judicial lawmaking to define the contours of acceptable gun control policy. Absent compelling evidence that is nowhere to be found in the Court's opinion, I could not possibly conclude that the Framers made such a choice.

For these reasons, I respectfully dissent.

7

Why Gun Makers Fear the NRA

BY PAUL M. BARRETT

In the days after the Sandy Hook Elementary School massacre on Dec. 14, 2012, executives with a half-dozen major U.S. gun manufacturers contacted the National Rifle Association. The firearm industry representatives didn't call the NRA, which they support with millions of dollars each year, to issue directives. On the contrary, they sought guidance on how to handle the public-relations crisis, according to people familiar with the situation who agreed to interviews on the condition they remain anonymous.

While the Obama administration had reacted meekly to mass shootings in Tucson and Aurora, Colo., Sandy Hook would be different. Twenty first-graders were dead. The president, a gun control supporter who previously had avoided the radioactive issue, wiped away tears when talking on television about the "beautiful little kids." As a nation, the normally stoic president added, "We have been through this too many times." In crass political terms, he was newly reelected and had less to lose in confronting pro-gun forces. The NRA's leadership faced a choice: Go to the mattresses as usual, or acknowledge the special horror of Sandy Hook and offer an olive branch.

That decision rested with Wayne LaPierre, the NRA's chief executive since 1991. One of Washington's most durable and enigmatic power brokers, LaPierre arrived at the organization in 1978 with a master's in political science from Boston College. The bookish Roanoke (Va.) native didn't know much about firearms. Colleagues joked that duck hunting with Wayne was more dangerous for the hunters than the ducks. Nevertheless, driven by an ambition impressive even by Washington standards, he rose swiftly, a mild-mannered presence in private who developed an Elmer Gantry-like persona for speeches and interviews.

In the immediate wake of Sandy Hook, the NRA reassured nervous gun company reps that they could stand down, according to people familiar with the situation. LaPierre would handle it.

One week after the massacre, he delivered a nationally televised tirade tinged with his trademark cultural resentment and paranoia. "Is the press and the political class here in Washington, D.C., so consumed by fear and hatred of the NRA and American gun owners," he said, "that you're willing to accept the world where real resistance to evil monsters is [an] unarmed school principal left to surrender her life, her life, to shield those children in her care?"

As intended, LaPierre's performance received massive media attention. It also upset many—including some gun makers. "The funerals were still going on in Newtown," says Joseph Bartozzi. "Parents were burying their children." A senior vice president at O.F. Mossberg & Sons, a shotgun and rifle manufacturer in North Haven, Conn., Bartozzi belongs to the NRA and applauds its stalwart defense of Second Amendment rights. But this time, LaPierre's diatribe struck him as ill-timed and graceless.

The companies that make and market firearms might prefer a softer tone, but they rarely complain publicly about NRA fear mongering because it's been so good for business. Corporate donations to the NRA, which together with its affiliates has annual revenue of $250 million, have risen during the past decade, a period when the organization has taken increasingly absolutist positions. Still, it's not the industry that muscles the NRA.

"NRA leadership worries about two things above all else: perpetuating controversy to stimulate fundraising from individual members and protecting its right flank from the real crazies," says Richard Feldman, author of a feisty 2007 memoir, *Ricochet: Confessions of a Gun Lobbyist*. Feldman has worked in various capacities for both the NRA and the industry. "The idea that the NRA follows orders from the gun companies is a joke," he says. "If anything, it's the other way around."

NRA spokesman Andrew Arulanandam declined to comment for this article, as did LaPierre and other top officials at the lobby group's Fairfax (Va.) headquarters. New York Mayor Michael Bloomberg, a gun control advocate, founded Bloomberg LP, which owns this magazine.

Gun companies defer to the NRA for two main reasons: First, there's intimidation. The lobby group has incited potentially ruinous consumer boycotts against firearm makers that fail to follow the NRA line with sufficient zeal. Second, regardless of some executives' concerns about civil discourse, gun companies benefit financially from the NRA's hype. Alarms about imminent gun confiscation—an NRA staple, despite its implausibility—reliably send firearm owners back to retail counters. Sales are booming. Mossberg is running three shifts a day. "Demand," Bartozzi says, "is very strong."

The two-story red brick Mossberg factory in North Haven stands behind barbed-wire-topped fencing just 25 miles east of Newtown, where the Sandy Hook children died, along with six educators. On the fatal morning, dazed company workers ran the production line with tears in their eyes. "They're neighbors," Bartozzi says. "Something like that, 20 little kids dead—what's the answer?"

Founded in 1919 and still owned by the wealthy Mossberg family, the company manufactures more pump-action shotguns than anyone else in the world. For generations, hunters, trap shooters, police departments, and the Pentagon have purchased its highly regarded weapons. In 2011, Mossberg began making the sort of large-capacity, military-style semiautomatic rifle used by the Newtown madman. The killer fired a Bushmaster Firearms International model, but it could just as easily have been a Mossberg. On the day I visited, a rack of black phosphate-finish MMR Tactical Rifles accommodating 30-round magazines awaited packaging and shipping near the loading dock. They retail for about $1,000 each.

Bartozzi, a former plant manager, has worked in the firearm industry for 33 years. He knew Sandy Hook would reignite gun control hostilities in Washington and the state capital of Hartford. "I get it," he says. "Politicians want to do something." Sure enough, Congress and Connecticut legislators were soon debating proposals to ban the sale of semiautomatics like those 30-round MMR Tactical Rifles. The instantly vicious tone of the debate, however, took even Bartozzi by surprise. The NRA, he says, should have "waited longer and tried to be more respectful of people who might disagree with them and still be struggling with grief."

Reaching out to those who disagree with him isn't the LaPierre way. A former legislative aide in the Virginia statehouse, he joined the NRA staff just after a brutal putsch by Second Amendment firebrands ousted the cadre of more reticent sportsmen who had traditionally dominated the group. The NRA made its first-ever presidential endorsement in 1980, when it backed Ronald Reagan. The sharper-edged gun organization joined conservative evangelicals and anti-abortion activists as ascendant players in the Reagan revolution.

Even after taking the NRA's helm in 1991, LaPierre fenced with the likes of Neal Knox, a lobbyist known for even more inflammatory, conspiracy views. Knox, who died eight years ago, insinuated in a gun periodical in 1994 that the assassinations of John and Robert Kennedy and Martin Luther King Jr. were part of a liberal plot to justify government confiscation of firearms.

LaPierre performed a remarkable high-wire act, trying to consolidate power, marginalize the Knoxites, and keep member contributions flowing. He became a "skilled hunter," according to the NRA's website. In 1995 he spiced a fundraising appeal with references to "federal agents wearing Nazi bucket helmets and black storm trooper uniforms" who "seize our guns, destroy our property, and even injure or kill us." Those comments struck some NRA members as over the line, especially after April 19, 1995, when insurrectionist Timothy McVeigh blew up an Oklahoma City building housing federal agents, killing 168 people. Former President George H. W. Bush quit the NRA in protest.

The Columbine (Colo.) high school massacre, which took 13 innocent lives in April 1999, prompted LaPierre to lean slightly in the other direction. At an NRA convention in Denver shortly afterward, he endorsed gun-free schools. "We believe in absolutely gun-free, zero-tolerance, totally safe schools," he told attendees. "That means no guns in America's schools, period." In congressional testimony, he urged lawmakers to expand the computerized Federal Bureau of Investigation background check system for sales by federally licensed retailers to cover "private" transactions at weekend gun shows and elsewhere.

LaPierre's Columbine response earned him no affection from gun control backers and mostly disdain from "the base," says Feldman, the former NRA operative. "Wayne took incredible grief among the more extreme elements, and he must have resolved, 'never again.'"

To understand LaPierre's reaction to Newtown, it's crucial to know that his organization does not possess a monopoly on the gun rights movement. Smaller, even more confrontational groups jostle with the NRA for attention and give LaPierre heartburn, say people who have worked with him over the years. Gun Owners of America, for example, calls itself "the only no-compromise gun lobby in Washington," an unsubtle dig at the NRA. Two days after the elementary school massacre, Larry Pratt, leader of the Springfield (Va.)-based GOA, jumped in front of LaPierre with a blistering op-ed in *USA Today*: "In addition to the gunman, blood is on the hands of members of Congress and the Connecticut legislators who voted to ban guns from all schools in Connecticut. They are the ones who made it illegal to defend oneself with a gun in a school." Pratt's group says it has 300,000 members; the NRA claimed 4 million before Newtown and says it has added hundreds of thousands since.

With Pratt on the warpath, LaPierre did not want to repeat what he saw in retrospect as his Columbine mistake, according to people present at the time. In his Dec. 21 appearance, he called for armed security in all schools, scorning gun-free classrooms as an enticement to "every insane killer in America that schools are their safest place to inflict maximum mayhem with minimum risk." More broadly, he described the country as plagued by surging bloodshed and dislocation. "Add another hurricane, terrorist attack, or some other natural or man-made disaster," he said, "and you've got a recipe for a national nightmare of violence and victimization."

Apocalyptic rhetoric reverberates through American gun rights circles. Matt Barber, vice president of Liberty Counsel Action, a Christian-right advocacy group, warned in a Jan. 11 article on the WorldNet-Daily website that by pushing gun control in the wake of Sandy Hook, Obama was "playing a very dangerous game of chicken" with firearm owners: "I fear this nation, already on the precipice of widespread civil unrest and economic disaster," he wrote, "might finally spiral into utter chaos, into a second civil war."

At a Jan. 20 Senate Judiciary Committee hearing, Chairman Patrick Leahy of Vermont noted that Second Amendment advocates have taken more extreme positions over the years. The Democratic senator asked LaPierre about his past support for background checks at gun shows. As with gun-free schools, LaPierre said that he had abandoned his earlier stance. Then he went further, condemning the background check system for licensed dealers: "I mean, we all know that homicidal maniacs, criminals, and the insane don't abide by the law."

That's not how a lot of the gun industry sounds. In mid-January, a month after Sandy Hook, the industry held its annual meet-and-greet, the SHOT (Shooting, Hunting, Outdoor Trade) Show in Las Vegas. In a keynote speech, Steve Sanetti, the president of the sponsoring trade association, the National Shooting Sports Foundation, boasted that the industry had helped invent computerized background checks in the 1980s, years before they became mandatory under federal law. "There have been 147 million background checks since 1998," he said proudly.

Sanetti, a former general counsel for gun manufacturer Sturm Ruger, didn't rail about the breakdown of law and order, let alone a second civil war. He stressed that the U.S. has a vibrant gun culture: "Over 300 million firearms are owned by almost half the households in America." (Gallup reports that "nearly 1 in 3 Americans personally owns a gun, and nearly half of households do.") "Firearm ownership among normal, law-abiding citizens has undeniably increased," he continued, "and over the last 30 years, despite the growth in firearm ownership, the homicide rate has declined by 50 percent, and violent crime has dramatically decreased to record lows not seen since the early 1960s." That's a far cry from Barber's or LaPierre's dystopia.

Over a couple of days, my interviews of executives and trade association officials at the SHOT expo revealed a significant patch of potential common ground between the industry and the Obama White House. There was little opposition to expanding background checks to cover private sales, a proposal that the administration has identified as its top priority. A beefed-up check system would not necessarily stop a determined mass killer, but proponents argue that it would provide a deterrent to a range of questionable transactions.

The businesspeople I spoke to in Las Vegas weren't brave about their views. Their not-for-attribution logic went like this: Licensed gun retailers, from giant Wal-Mart Stores to mom-and-pop Main Street shops, already do background checks. These gun sellers would not mind seeing their unlicensed dealer competition forced to comply with the same rules. Most gun manufacturers, meanwhile, are agnostic on the issue. They sell their products to wholesalers, which in turn do business with licensed dealers.

On March 5, 2012, the *Washington Post* quoted Sanetti as saying that comprehensive background checks "are more the NRA's issue." He added: "From the commercial side, we're already there, and we've been there, and we were the ones that have been the strongest proponents of an effective, complete background check." The same day, Sanetti clamorously retreated in a press release, saying that the newspaper "incorrectly implies" that his statement put him at odds with the NRA.

The gun industry has not always been so timid. For a brief period in the 1990s, executives at some companies rethought their relationship with the NRA. Feldman says LaPierre's likening federal agents to Nazis particularly stirred apprehension. "Gun companies wanted to sell guns to law-abiding citizens and cops. They didn't want to be associated with McVeigh and the black-helicopter crowd," he says.

In October 1997, senior executives from Smith & Wesson, Glock, and other handgun manufacturers trooped to the White House Rose Garden for a photo op with Bill Clinton—a gesture of cooperation with a Democratic president unimaginable today. Feldman, then the executive director of a trade group called the American Shooting Sports Council, had orchestrated the televised event. Clinton praised the gun companies for volunteering to ship a trigger lock with every handgun. The manufacturers did so as an alternative to a proposed federal lock mandate. Before the ceremony, Feldman joked with Clinton that there would be hell to pay from the NRA: "I want to thank you, Mr. President," Feldman recalls saying, "for offering to find me a spot in the federal witness protection program." Clinton chuckled.

LaPierre was not amused. He sent a vitriolic open letter to the executives who visited the Rose Garden. "Firearm safety—as it's being pressed by the Administration—is a phony," LaPierre wrote. "It is simply a stalking horse for gun bans." Rather than herald an era of gun control détente, the Rose Garden episode turned out to be the high point of tension between gun makers and the NRA. In 1998 and 1999, gun control activists working with big-city mayors and the Clinton administration launched a series of lawsuits against the industry en masse—an attempt to imitate earlier litigation against cigarette manufacturers. While the much larger tobacco companies could afford to settle (ultimately for $246 billion to be paid over a quarter-century), the U.S. gun industry at the time had total annual sales of only about $1.3 billion. Defense lawyer fees alone threatened some firearm companies' financial viability.

This created an opening for the NRA. "Your fight has become our fight," ex-Hollywood star Charlton Heston, then the group's ceremonial president, told executives at the winter 1999 SHOT Show. In 2000, when Smith & Wesson tried to resolve its liability problems by negotiating a truce with the Clinton administration, under which S&W agreed to unprecedented federal regulation, the NRA helped incite a consumer boycott that nearly destroyed the company. Smith & Wesson renounced its settlement and was readmitted to the fold. The NRA then pressed successfully for state and federal statutes that summarily extinguished the municipal lawsuits.

Along the way, most gun companies, with the NRA's encouragement, branded the wheeler-dealer Feldman persona non grata and shut down his trade group. Today he leads a small organization called the Independent Firearm Owners Association, which promotes gun rights but also backs expanded background checks. "I think you could say that the industry learned a lesson," Feldman says: "If you cross the NRA, you will pay for it."

Having rescued the gun companies from death by lawsuit, the NRA informed the industry in 2005 that a reward would be appropriate. Over the next six years, various companies donated a total of between $14.7 million and $38.9 million, according to the pro-gun control Violence Policy Center, which analyzed NRA records. About three-quarters of NRA corporate donors came from the firearm industry, others from fields such as insurance and advertising.

The corporate generosity continues. During the past year, the NRA has welcomed Smith & Wesson to its Ring of Freedom program for donations exceeding $1 million. At the NRA's annual meeting last year in St. Louis, Sturm Ruger presented a check for $1.25 million.

Drawing on the Violence Policy Center's research, activist groups such as MoveOn.org have focused their post-Newtown politicking "on who the NRA really is and who really calls the shots, which is the gun companies," according to Garlin Gilchrist II. MoveOn's Washington-based national campaign director, Gilchrist adds that the NRA "is the mechanism by which the gun industry is spreading the money around to block common-sense reforms and preserve loopholes in existing laws." In an online campaign called "The NRA Doesn't Speak for Me," MoveOn is promoting gun owners who favor greater restrictions. "We've never seen a reaction from our members like this on any issue," Gilchrist says. MoveOn has raised nearly $1 million in donations on the gun issue since Jan. 1.

By accelerating its corporate buck-raking, the NRA opened itself to MoveOn's critique. The question, though, is whether liberals accomplished anything other than gathering money and mirroring their foe's conspiracy talk.

Corporate dollars, moreover, still make up only a modest fraction of the NRA's budget. Most of its money comes from individual dues and contributions, ads sold by NRA publications, and merchandise. During a Jan. 13, 2012 interview with CNN, David Keene, the NRA's president, said corporate fundraising will continue, adding: "We get less money from the industry than we'd like to get."

Mossberg doesn't appear on the NRA's roster of the top 93 corporate donors, but it does promote NRA membership to its customers. The Mossberg family typically keeps a low profile, and its company doesn't disclose its financial results. Bartozzi will say that, like the rest of the industry, his employer has been enjoying strong revenue, in part because of the "Obama surge," a buying spree that began in late 2008 in response to the NRA's warnings that President Obama eventually would make it more difficult to acquire certain guns. Industrywide sales for 2011 were $4.3 billion, up 30 percent since 2008. "We have shown a year-over-year increase in sales for several years," Bartozzi says. He expresses gratitude to the NRA. The group, he says, "protects Second Amendment rights, and those rights protect the ability to buy our products."

The current round of gun control debates would have had less effect on Mossberg had the company not begun, in 2011, to manufacture the military-style rifles referred to within the industry as AR-15s or, by gun opponents, as assault weapons. "We're late to the AR game," Bartozzi says. "We sell those because that's what people want. Our customers drive our decisions." Mossberg invested $4 million last year in plant improvements, largely to accommodate its AR-15 products for hunting and law enforcement. Industrywide, some 4 million AR-15s have sold in the past decade.

Bartozzi frames his arguments in practical terms. He doesn't expect bans of military-style weapons or large magazines to pass Congress. The Connecticut legislature is another story. The NRA and the Connecticut Citizens Defense League organized popular opposition to the state curbs, including a rally in Hartford that featured a caricature of Governor Malloy as a British redcoat with a proclamation that it's "1775 all over again." Connecticut gun executives, including Bartozzi and officials with Colt's Manufacturing, based in the state since the mid-19th century, lobbied in less emotional terms. In an interview, Bartozzi suggested that Connecticut companies should get an exemption from any legislation that would allow them to continue manufacturing AR-15s, even if in-state sales of the rifles became illegal. Such an anomaly seems odd: Go ahead and build the weapons, but make sure to sell them elsewhere. Bartozzi says it would be justified, in part, because of Connecticut's special role in firearm history. "Eli Whitney started the American gun industry in Connecticut in the 1700s," he says. "It would be a shame to destroy that good and long history. Also, Connecticut needs the jobs."

The Mossbergs reside in the state and want the company to continue operating there, he says. But depending on the regulatory landscape, the family will have to consider moving more, or all, of its operations to a Mossberg plant in Eagle Pass, Tex., which already employs a majority of the company's 670 workers.

"We know we're going to get some kind of legislation in Connecticut," Bartozzi says. "All we're asking is that we be at the table to lend our expertise and work out a way for people to keep making firearms in this state. Otherwise, we'll just make them somewhere else."

8

How Police Justify Shootings: The 1974 Killing of an Unarmed Teen Set a Standard

BY JANELL ROSS

It was late, just before 10:45 p.m., in Memphis, Tennessee. A neighbor called the police to report a possible break-in at the house next door.

When Officer Elton Hymon, who is black, and his partner arrived at the house, Hymon saw a figure dash through the backyard and start to climb a chain-link fence, according to court records. Hymon yelled, "Halt, police!" With his flashlight, Hymon could see that the figure wasn't armed, but the person kept climbing, so Hymon fired a single shot. It struck the back of the person's head, splattering his brain across the fence.

When the officers reached the fence, they found Edward Garner, who was just 15 years old and weighed only 110 pounds. He was carrying a wallet stolen from the house. It contained $10.

Edward, who was black, died in October 1974, but a lawsuit filed by his father went all the way to the U.S. Supreme Court and set an important standard for what justifies a police shooting. Many of the elements of the case, the questions it prompted and the statements police and community activists made afterward could easily be mistaken for events in 2020. They remain relevant in a country that continues to grapple with a rate of police shootings far higher than those of other developed countries.

Edward's father sued the Memphis Police Department. The case, *Tennessee v. Garner*, led to a 1985 Supreme Court decision in the family's favor that established that police can't shoot fleeing suspects unless they pose immediate danger. For many states, the Garner decision set the first legal standard for police shootings since the 19th century, shifting notions of propriety in law enforcement and, for a time, reducing the number of people shot and killed by police.

"It set the standard, defined a kind of boundary for contemporary lawful policing," said Hank Fradella, a lawyer and professor in the School of Criminology and Criminal Justice at Arizona State University.

But police shootings have continued, including one in Vallejo, California, which faced new scrutiny after video was released. In the decades since the Garner decision, the names of Edward Garner and his father — who pursued justice for an imperfect son — have faded into obscurity. Indeed, the names of many who forced the country and its most senior legal minds to think more deeply about police decisions to shoot and kill aren't widely known.

And while *Tennessee v. Garner* became a fixture of police training, the standard it set also taught officers what they needed to say and do to legally justify shooting a suspect. Of the 1,000 people police kill on average every year, a disproportionate number are black. (In 2019, 23 percent of those killed by police were black; black Americans make up just 13 percent of the population.)

The Garner case, then, has left a mixed legacy, according to experts in policing, as well as people directly involved in bringing the lawsuit decades ago.

"I don't know that the Supreme Court saying we are going to limit police officers' ability to use deadly force against fleeing suspects means there were changes," Fradella said. "I don't know whether that's enough to overcome perceptions of danger, the potential for danger officers feel. I don't think a case actually changes human behavior that much."

A DETERMINATION TO CHANGE THINGS

When Edward was killed, Tennessee's law allowing police to shoot fleeing violent crime suspects — using any "necessary means" to stop them — dated to 1858.

Edward's father, Cleamtee Garner, was well acquainted with the ways the government can malfunction and leave black Americans in particular peril. He was born in Memphis in 1919, in what the journalist Ida B. Wells would call "The Red Summer," a year when white mobs lynched, burned alive, maimed and terrorized thousands of black people in nearly 40 cities. Hundreds died.

As a young man, Cleamtee Garner fought in World War II, earning the American Campaign Medal and the American Defense Medal. He came home to a country so eager to maintain white supremacy that black veterans returning from foreign service, aware of life outside the segregated United States, became frequent targets of violent white attacks. They represented a large number of those lynched and were denied benefits owed them under the GI Bill.

Edward was the youngest of Cleamtee and Bertha Garner's seven children, a fourth and much beloved son.

A few weeks after Edward's death, Cleamtee Garner visited the office of Walter Bailey, a black Memphis lawyer. Garner, who worked as a packer at the Memphis Defense Distribution Depot, arrived in a suit and tie, sad but certain about what he wanted to do: sue the police department and the officer who shot his son.

"Mr. Garner was a very regular working man, with a strong sense that what happened here was not only wrong, but emblematic of the way this city was policed at the time," Bailey, 79, said in an interview.

In 1974, Memphis was where, just six years earlier, Martin Luther King Jr. had been assassinated on a motel balcony. Three years after that, eight police officers and sheriff's deputies were acquitted in the beating death of a 17-year-old black boy after falsely claiming that he had been fatally injured in a car crash while fleeing police.

Bailey was one of just a few black lawyers working in Memphis at one of the South's first integrated law firms. It often did legal work for activists and the NAACP. He'd pursued and lost two cases against the Memphis police. At the moment King was shot, Bailey was in a Memphis law library researching how to fight a court order barring King from a march in support of Memphis' black sanitation workers.

By 1974, black people in Memphis were frustrated and infuriated by unchecked police mistreatment and abuse — but many were also afraid, Bailey said. It was a situation not entirely different from the one black Americans face around the country today. Police prosecutions remain rare.

Cleamtee Garner, who died in 1994, was determined to change things. He told Bailey that he knew his son had done something wrong. He would have encouraged Edward to accept a just verdict and, if ordered, jail time. But the penalty for burglary in the United States, for making off with $10, shouldn't be immediate death.

'WE ASSUMED WE WERE GOING TO LOSE'

Bailey believed the Garner case included possible violations of the Fourth Amendment, the right of people to be free from unreasonable searches and seizures. He told Garner that he would take the case but that it might take some time.

The case first went to a federal court in Memphis, where Garner and Bailey lost. Garner agreed that Bailey should appeal. When they won the appeal, Tennessee took the case to the Supreme Court. Bailey handled the case in the lower courts, but now the NAACP Legal Defense and Education Fund would do so.

Steven Winter was just 31 when he found himself on a small team arguing the Garner case before the Supreme Court in 1984.

"We assumed we were going to lose," said Winter, who is now a constitutional law professor at Wayne State University in Detroit.

Winter, who is white, argued that the FBI's use-of-force standard — shoot in situations in which a threat is imminent and immediate self-defense or defense of others is necessary — represented a better model than Tennessee's law allowing police to shoot fleeing violent crime suspects. And burglary was a property crime, not a violent one, he argued. In the early 1980s, only about 1.5 percent of burglaries involved any confrontation between burglar and resident, an NAACP researcher found. And, in most of those cases, that amounted to shouting matches, not violence.

The day of the 1985 Supreme Court decision, Winter picked up the phone for his only conversation with Garner.

"I told him he had won, that after 11 long years he had won at the U.S. Supreme Court," Winter said. "We had a very interesting conversation. I know I said we won on the legal issue, but it has to go back down to the lower court on the damage issue," which would determine whether Garner would receive a payout from the city.

"I said that I was sorry but there would not be any kind of compensation soon," Winter continued. "And Mr. Garner said to me, 'I don't care about the money, just so they don't shoot no more kids.'"

The Garner case meant officers could shoot fleeing suspects only as a last resort to protect the life of an officer or a bystander. The decision became a front-page story in The New York Times. Cleamtee Garner wasn't quoted.

In 1995, 21 years after Edward Garner's death and 10 years after the Supreme Court decision, Bailey persuaded the city of Memphis to settle with the Garner family for $300,000, plus $145,000 in legal and court fees. But Cleamtee Garner, 74, died 15 months before the case could be resolved and was buried with military honors in Memphis National Cemetery.

'IT FOREVER ALTERED POLICING'

The Garner case toppled the notion that police could shoot and kill people who posed no immediate threat.

In the year following the Supreme Court decision, police shot and killed about 57 fewer people than would have been expected, according to a study published in the Journal of Criminal Law and Criminology in 1994, based on national homicide data. Within the first few years after the decision, in states that once allowed police to shoot fleeing suspects, fatal police shootings dropped by almost 24 percent, compared to almost 13 percent in other states, the study found.

"Garner unquestionably changed the way that police officers in Memphis and around the country understood that they were supposed to handle different situations," said Michael Rallings, Memphis' police director. "It forever altered policing."

Rallings, who is black, joined the Memphis Police Department in 1990. Rallings remembers sessions during his time in the police academy about the Garner case led by the city's district attorney. It remains part of the curriculum today, along with two more recent Supreme Court cases dealing with the use of force and fleeing suspects.

To Rallings, both Bailey and Hymon, the officer who shot Edward, merit recognition.

Bailey pressed the case for decades. Hymon went into court and told the truth about what he saw and did. Last year, Rallings invited both men to speak with Memphis' senior officers.

Bailey accepted and spoke about how the Garner case saved lives. Hymon didn't.

Hymon retired from the Memphis Police Department in 2009 as a captain and became a full-time minister. He and several of Cleamtee Garner's surviving children didn't respond to multiple requests for comment.

But in February 2019, Hymon granted a rare interview to a black Memphis-area newspaper, The New Tri-State Defender. Hymon had joined the police department the year before he shot and killed Edward. He found the department's 1970s-era culture troubling. White officers often uttered the n-word, and some notched their guns for every black person they'd killed, Hymon said. Many white officers also carried a "drop gun" to plant on a suspect so use of deadly force wouldn't be questioned. That issue came up at the Supreme Court during the Garner case.

After killing an unarmed 15-year-old boy, a routine suspension and an investigation, Hymon "returned to a hero's reception," he told the reporter.

"What I resented," he added, "was the implication that after killing an African American I was acceptable."

A CONTINUING PROBLEM

Researchers have long noted that when a police department changes its use-of-force policy, officers correspondingly change how they describe events. For example, in Memphis after the Garner decision, the number of shootings described as having occurred while working to "apprehend suspect" declined by 58.6 percent, while the rate of shootings described as necessary to "defend life" increased by 91.5 percent, according to the Journal of Criminal Law and Criminology research.

Police seemed to grasp the Garner ruling and became more adept at describing their actions in the terms most likely to be deemed justifiable, Winter said. And when the Supreme Court later handed down decisions that emphasized a different standard for use of force — what a reasonable police officer would do — police shootings began to climb.

Other factors influence decision-making by officers. Among them: officers' conscious and unconscious biases; myths that have permeated police culture about a zone of safety, or the distance that must be maintained from suspects who pose a threat; reduced emphasis on tactics and more emphasis on dominance and control; and the average six months' training time new officers get before they're typically placed on late-night shifts in high-crime districts, the most challenging work environments.

Police shootings, while more plentiful in the United States than in other countries, are still relatively rare. But those factors, along with the Supreme Court's most recent case involving a fleeing suspect in 2007, have created conditions under which police shootings are a leading cause of death for young men.

And the 1,000 people, on average, killed by police every year continue to include unarmed, fleeing individuals, a disproportionate share of whom are black. Many come with complications that their families and police view in very different ways.

In 2014, a Cleveland police officer shot and killed a 12-year-old black boy in a city park after a witness reported that the boy was playing with what the witness said may have been a toy gun. The officers drove their police cruiser onto the park's grass, stopping within feet of the boy and shot and killed him within seconds. The officers weren't told that the item in the boy's hand may have been a toy, and they weren't indicted.

In October 2019, a Fort Worth, Texas, police officer shot and killed a 28-year-old black woman after entering her yard, failing to identify himself and then firing through her window without warning. Police say the woman was armed. The officer has been charged with murder.

And this week, officials in Vallejo, California, released video that they say shows an off-duty police officer from a nearby city shooting and killing an armed 38-year-old black man after an argument over a parking space in November. Vallejo police have described the shooting as an act of legal self-defense. The officer hasn't been charged, but the investigation continues. The dead man's family has sued.

To Winter, the continued spate of police shootings shows the need for a stronger standard for what makes a shooting justifiable.

"As big a deal as Garner was, I'm afraid that Trevor Noah, the 'Daily Show' [host], is right," Winter said. "He said the way things currently stand for black Americans is: 'If you don't show your hands, you get shot. You show your hands, you get shot. You have a legal gun, you get shot. You don't, very likely get shot.' Garner was massive, but its impact and influence has faded with time."

PART III

WHAT DO WE NOW

9

The Christchurch Call Summit

BY JACINDA ARDERN, AMAZON, FACEBOOK, GOOGLE, MICROSOFT, AND TWITTER

On May 15, 2019, Jacinda Ardern and Emmanuel Macron held the Christchurch Call Summit in Paris, France, two months after the Christchurch mosque shooting in New Zealand. The aim of the summit was to bring countries together and change social media so that it would not promote and facilitate extremist terrorism.

This is the speech that New Zealand Prime Minister Jacinda Ardern delivered, followed by the resolutions jointly adopted by Amazon, Facebook, Google, Microsoft, and Twitter.

Kia ora koutou katoa and warm greetings from Aotearoa, New Zealand.

Many of you will have come today from the Tech for Good Summit. Others will have been present at what has been called the Christchurch Call.

Essentially, our motivations have been the same—to create change for the better.

In the wake of the terrorist attack in Christchurch New Zealand on the 15th of March, you may have seen many images or footage.

Disturbingly, you may have also seen the attack itself.

Not because social media was created to be a platform for violence—but because a man thousands of miles away from here used its openness and accessibility to spread hate.

In doing so he not only violated the standards set for those platforms, he violated our most basic sense of humanity.

But there were other images you may not have seen.

Like the one of a group of young people who answered the call from a local student leader that lost pupils in the attack to gather together in a show of solidarity and mourning with our Muslim community.

Or the ones of an anti-racism rallies, or those of memorials organized hastily and organically all around New Zealand in the days after the 15th of March.

All over New Zealand groups came together because they were connected to one another by social media. Connected for good.

For every example of hate, there is an example of good. But we run the risk of diminishing the positive elements of technology if we simply accept that one will be a necessary part of the other. That an open and accessible internet simply means that extremism will coexist in the same space.

I do not except that, and the participation of many of you in the Christchurch Call tells me that neither do you.

The Christchurch Call to action, which was agreed today, has a simple premise. That tech companies have both enormous power, and enormous responsibility. And so do governments. We each have a role to play in protecting an open, free and secure internet, and in protecting the freedom of expression.

But this has never and should never be used as a justification for leaving extremism and terrorism unchecked.

No one after all has the right to broadcast murder.

And so today we came together to make a start.

We pledged to each undertake a series of steps to prevent the proliferation of this kind of harmful content online.

We undertook to keep looking for the technological solutions that will make a difference, as well as the regulatory ones.

We acknowledged that we can do more by collaborating than we can alone, and that while there will be areas where we disagree and challenge each other, there will also be areas where we agree.

The same could be said for so many of the challenges we face as an international community.

Digital disruption, inequality, the future of work, right through to climate change—the biggest issue of mine and President Macron's generation and the generation to come—technology has a significant and powerful role to play for each of these challenges.

For that to happen, we each have to play our part.

For our part as governments, we can be enablers and collaborators.

Provide an environment where technology can thrive and so too the creators and innovators.

Create the space to ask questions and to debate solutions rather than shout each other down.

At the same time, technology companies can continue to seek solutions to our most pressing challenges while civil society guides us in our duty of care to seek solutions that don't undermine basic rights and freedoms.

I'd like to think the Christchurch Call has tried to model this approach.

To those who came to join us for this express purpose from Senegal, Indonesia, Canada, Norway, Ireland, Jordan, the United Kingdom and European Union, I thank you for your leadership.

To President Macron, I called you some six weeks ago with a view on what we needed to do in the wake of the terrorist attack we experienced, and you have been a willing and open partner. My express gratitude to you for your leadership.

And to each of us. As humans, we are all here and motivated possibly by different things.

Whether it's your belief in the power of these new technologies to organize and unite, the ability to solve problems, the power of being able to freely express an idea that can be amplified beyond your own borders.

For me, well my motivation is simple.

To never ever again have to stand in front of a group of young people who were amongst the millions who saw the indiscriminate murder of 51 members of their communities, knowing that we could have done something to prevent that.

There are solutions, we just need to commit to finding them.

Thank you for being a part of that.

No reira, tēnā koutou, tēnā koutou, tēnā tatou katoa.

THE CHRISTCHURCH CALL AND STEPS TO TACKLE TERRORIST AND VIOLENT EXTREMIST CONTENT FROM AMAZON, FACEBOOK, GOOGLE, MICROSOFT, AND TWITTER

In addition to signing the Christchurch Call, Amazon, Facebook, Google, Twitter and Microsoft are publishing nine steps that they will take to address the abuse of technology to spread terrorist and violent extremist content. These nine steps include five individual actions that each company is committing to take, and a further four collaborative actions they'll take together. Here are the nine steps:

Actions to address the abuse of technology to spread terrorist and violent extremist content

As online content sharing service providers, we commit to the following:

FIVE INDIVIDUAL ACTIONS

Terms of Use. We commit to updating our terms of use, community standards, codes of conduct, and acceptable use policies to expressly prohibit the distribution of terrorist and violent extremist content. We believe this is important to establish baseline expectations for users and to articulate a clear basis for removal of this content from our platforms and services and suspension or closure of accounts distributing such content.

User Reporting of Terrorist and Violent Extremist Content. We commit to establishing one or more methods within our online platforms and services for users to report or flag inappropriate content, including terrorist and violent extremist content. We will ensure that the reporting mechanisms are clear, conspicuous, and easy to use, and provide enough categorical granularity to allow the company to prioritize and act promptly upon notification of terrorist or violent extremist content.

Enhancing Technology. We commit to continuing to invest in technology that improves our capability to detect and remove terrorist and violent extremist content online, including the extension or development of digital fingerprinting and AI-based technology solutions.

Livestreaming. We commit to identifying appropriate checks on livestreaming, aimed at reducing the risk of disseminating terrorist and violent extremist content online. These may include enhanced vetting measures (such as streamer ratings or scores, account activity, or validation processes) and moderation of certain livestreaming events where appropriate. Checks on livestreaming necessarily will be tailored to the context of specific livestreaming services, including the type of audience, the nature or character of the livestreaming service, and the likelihood of exploitation.

Transparency Reports. We commit to publishing on a regular basis transparency reports regarding detection and removal of terrorist or violent extremist content on our online platforms and services and ensuring that the data is supported by a reasonable and explainable methodology.

FOUR COLLABORATIVE ACTIONS

Shared Technology Development. We commit to working collaboratively across industry, governments, educational institutions, and NGOs to develop a shared understanding of the contexts in which terrorist and violent extremist content is published and to improve technology to detect and remove terrorist and violent extremist content more effectively and efficiently. This will include:

- Work to create robust shared data sets to accelerate machine learning and AI and sharing insights and learnings from the data.

- Development of open source or other shared tools to detect and remove terrorist or violent extremist content.

- Enablement of all companies, large and small, to contribute to the collective effort and to better address detection and removal of this content on their platforms and services.

Crisis Protocols. We commit to working collaboratively across industry, governments, and NGOs to create a protocol for responding to emerging or active events, on an urgent basis, so relevant information can be quickly and efficiently shared, processed, and acted upon by all stakeholders with minimal delay. This includes the establishment of incident management teams that coordinate actions and broadly distribute information that is in the public interest.

Education. We commit to working collaboratively across industry, governments, educational institutions, and NGOs to help understand and educate the public about terrorist and extremist violent content online. This includes educating and reminding users about how to report or otherwise not contribute to the spread of this content online.

Combatting Hate and Bigotry. We commit to working collaboratively across industry to attack the root causes of extremism and hate online. This includes providing greater support for relevant research – with an emphasis on the impact of online hate on offline discrimination and violence – and supporting capacity and capability of NGOs working to challenge hate and promote pluralism and respect online.

10

How People Can Take on the NRA

BY COMMON CAUSE

INTRODUCTION

After a lone gunman killed 14 students and three faculty members and wounded more than a dozen others at Marjory Stoneman Douglas High School in Parkland, FL, on Valentine's Day, young survivors of the massacre resolved to tackle the formidable power of the gun lobby across America.

In just a few weeks, the Parkland students have captured the nation's imagination and brought new energy into the long running efforts to regulate gun ownership. They've pushed the Florida legislature and Gov. Rick Scott to tighten the state's gun laws, faced down the president at the White House, and led their fellow students at thousands of high schools across the country in a dramatic, peaceful walkout to demand stronger laws to protect their lives. Now they're planning a mammoth "March for Our Lives" down Pennsylvania Avenue in Washington, DC, with sibling marches in cities and towns throughout the country and around the globe to demand that lives and safety "become a priority and that we end gun violence and mass shootings in our schools today."

Gun violence is now a leading cause of death in the United States. Every year on average, more than 35,000 people die from gun violence, and another 81,000 survive after being shot, according to the Brady Campaign to Prevent Gun Violence.[1] The violence disproportionally affects communities of color; black men are 13 times more likely than white men to be shot and killed by a gun[2] and black children die from gun-related homicides at a rate ten times that of white children, according to a study by the Centers of Disease Control and Prevention.[3]

The death tolls from single-day mass shootings continue to reach new records. Last year, 58 concertgoers died and another 500 were injured at a country music festival in Las Vegas. The year before, 49 people were shot to death and another 50 injured at an Orlando LGBTQ nightclub. Those mass shootings surpassed the death tolls of the Virginia Tech massacre, which left 32 college students and professors dead in 2007, and the 2012 Sandy Hook Elementary School shooting, in which 20 children – ages six and seven – and six teachers were murdered in what President Obama called the single worst day of his presidency.

Various policies to tighten gun laws enjoy wide support. According to a February 2018 poll by Quinnipiac University, "support for universal background checks, a mandatory waiting period for firearm purchases, and an assault weapon ban came in at 97%, 83%, and 67% respectively."[4]

If our political system worked as intended, with everyone enjoying an equal voice in the decisions that affect our lives, our families and our communities, such a combination of facts, backed by public opinion, already would have yielded substantial changes in our gun laws.

But the truth is that our system has been thrown out of balance by the power of moneyed interests, including the gun lobby and the weapons industry. In many places – especially Congress – many with the power to act instead express their "thoughts and prayers" and move on without making any substantive changes to our laws.

Many cite the National Rifle Association's political spending as an explanation for our elected leaders' intransigence on this issue. And with good reason – the NRA boasts that it has 5 million members (a number that some dispute) and spends tens of millions of dollars on politics.[5] But as this report makes clear, the NRA's power goes beyond its campaign spending. It has created a sophisticated grassroots operation to push its agenda in statehouses and in Congress.

The NRA's political influence, however, is no match for the power of the American voter – provided we make our voices heard at every election, and if we solve some underlying governance challenges that skew policy in favor of wealthy special interests.

This report examines critical aspects of the NRA's perceived influence, and is intended to suggest solutions that will rebalance power to ensure that our democracy is responsive to our needs. This report does not recommend specific policies to reduce gun violence – but proposes solutions to boost the political power of Americans of every political persuasion – including the overwhelming number of people who support changes to our gun laws to save lives.

THE NRA'S ORGANIZING & MEMBERSHIP BASE

Voters hold the ultimate power in a democracy. Organized voters have more power than unorganized ones. The NRA's influence and political success extends beyond campaign contributions and independent expenditures and into political organizing and mobilizing of a grassroots base of voters who are known to vote frequently and follow the recommendations of the organization.

Key to the power of the NRA and its affiliates is their grassroots base. The NRA claims "nearly five million members,"[6] but this number is impossible to verify and the organization has an interest in reporting an inflated or high-end estimate (including active "lifetime" memberships from deceased individuals).[7] Still, the NRA's membership is perceived by lawmakers as a powerful force that can be mobilized to support – or defeat – legislation and candidates.

The opinions of NRA members do not necessarily match perfectly with the policies the NRA promotes. While some NRA members join the organization because they support the policy goals and political advocacy, many others join for the extensive benefits and services provided – including discounted insurance, access to private clubs, a print magazine, and firearms safety classes, to name a few. This helps grow the NRA's membership ranks and creates a cycle of membership engagement from lifestyle (discounts and a magazine) to politics.[8] After the shooting in Parkland, however, a number of the NRA's corporate partners have re-evaluated their relationship with the organization.[9] It may have a long-term impact.

Individuals can become leaders within the NRA as firearms instructors or coaches. With 125,000 instructors[10] (training 1 million people each year) the NRA gives volunteers a significant role in building the organization. NRA members may have joined for the discounts, but are constantly recruited to take leadership roles, as well as join in political activities supporting the NRA leadership's positions.

There's strong evidence that the NRA's policy and lobbying priorities reflect the priorities of gun manufacturers more than rank-and-file members.

The gun industry relies on the NRA's lobbying power as a "de facto trade association" according to one expert.[11] Opposition to expanded background checks – and other measures like raising the minimum age to buy a long gun or assault rifle – are priorities of the gun industry, which will see its profits shrink with these reforms. But multiple surveys (including from prominent Republican pollster Frank Luntz[12]) have found that about three in four NRA members surveyed support universal criminal background checks of anyone purchasing a gun,[13] a policy the NRA vehemently opposes.[14] The NRA's letter-grade system reinforces a no-compromise approach to political advocacy with the threat that NRA members will vote out of office any official who doesn't receive an "A" grade.[15] Even if NRA members personally agree with policies like universal background checks, the industry opposition is reflected in the letter grades of candidates.

Even if a majority of NRA members demanded change, the structure and bylaws of the organization might prevent it. Only those who have been NRA members for at least five years (or have signed up for a lifetime membership) can vote in NRA elections. And NRA officials and members who cross Executive Vice President Wayne LaPierre, who is close with the gun industry, are forced out or marginalized.[16]

The large media presence of the NRA (seven print and online magazines, popular YouTube and other social media channels) also helps it recruit new members and highlights the importance of its political activities. With a constant barrage of stories and commentary that vilifies the NRA's political opponents and reinforces a feeling that the freedom of gun owners is under attack from powerful forces, the NRA membership is primed and motivated to vote. Some of the NRA's recent digital videos evince extreme hostility to the media, echoing President Trump's attacks on journalists and a free press.

Building a grassroots base of support takes significant resources. The NRA paid more than $20 million in 2015 to a single membership-building vendor.[17] Its corporate ties also help the organization build its membership. The NRA's funding comes from membership dues, plus donations from gun manufacturers and political interest groups; the latter group includes the Koch family-backed Freedom Partners, which contributed about $5 million to the NRA in 2014.[18] While the NRA doesn't release details on donations from gun industry players, independent analysis by the Violence Policy Center shows that since 2005, "corporate partners" (in NRA parlance) have donated between $19.3 million and $60.2 million to the organization.[19] One gun company, MidwayUSA, proudly states on its website that it has donated nearly $15 million to the NRA.[20] The NRA also receives millions from the gun industry to advertise their products in NRA publications.[21] And gun manufacturer Taurus provides a free NRA membership with each purchase.[22]

NRA'S ELECTION SPENDING

Of the groups and organizations that promote the interests of the gun industry, the NRA is by far the biggest political spender.

Its spending has increased significantly in recent years. Empowered by the Supreme Court's decision in Citizens United and other cases, the NRA spends more money every election cycle to elect candidates who will do its bidding and support its policy agenda, and defeat those who won't. And importantly, it also can threaten to spend money for and against candidates. The threat alone can advance or stall policy because elected officials fear that the NRA will spend whatever it takes to defeat them.

Since 1989, the NRA – measured by money from its PACs and employees – has contributed approximately $23 million directly to federal candidates, parties, and other political committees, according to the Center for Responsive Politics.[23] Its money almost exclusively supports Republicans. NRA allies like Safari Club International, the National Shooting Sports Foundation, and Gun Owners of America make the bulk of other pro-gun donations, for a grand total of $42 million from the pro-gun lobby since 1989.[24]

At the state level, the NRA has contributed at least $17 million to state candidates and committees since 1990, according to data made available by the National Institute on Money in State Politics.[25] Spending by the pro-gun lobby is exceptionally more than that of groups that favor tighter gun laws – the latter have spent only $4.3 million since 1989.[26]

But direct contributions per election cycle are only a drop in the NRA's campaign bucket.

The NRA spends most of its election money on "independent expenditures" – not campaign contributions. Often, these take the form of paid advertisements calling for the election or defeat of candidates.

The NRA greatly boosted its independent spending after the Supreme Court decided Citizens United in 2010; that ruling declared that corporations – including some nonprofits like the NRA – have a constitutional right to spend unlimited amounts to influence elections.

In the 2016 federal election cycle alone, the NRA spent at least $54 million on independent expenditures in federal elections — $37 million against Democrats, $17.3 million for Republicans, and only $265 for Democrats.[27] That is nearly double the $27 million it spent during the 2014 midterms and more than double the $19 million it spent in the 2012 presidential election.[28] The NRA's independent expenditures are far higher than the $3 million in independent spending by groups advocating stricter gun laws in 2016, and the $8.6 million those groups spent in 2014.[29]

The Supreme Court has affirmed that Americans have a right to know who is spending money to influence their votes and their views. Eight justices endorsed the importance of disclosure in Citizens United, even as the rest of the opinion (which only had the support of five justices) demonstrated how out of touch the Court is with how campaigns are run by incorrectly assuming that adequate disclosure already exists.

"The court declared, 'With the advent of the Internet, prompt disclosure of expenditures can provide shareholders and citizens with the information needed to hold corporations and elected officials accountable for their positions and supporters.' It also said that disclosure 'permits citizens and shareholders to react to the speech of corporate entities in a proper way. This transparency enables the electorate to make informed decisions and give proper weight to different speakers and messages.' And the court expressed enthusiasm that technology today makes disclosure 'rapid and informative.' What went wrong? The court's vision of disclosure and transparency is nowhere in sight. In fact, campaign finance in the United States has, by many measures, fallen into an era dominated by 'dark money,' with donors hiding in the shadows and hundreds of millions of dollars of contributions flowing through politics without a trace of who gave it or why." Washington Post Editorial Board, January 20, 2015

Unfortunately, any comprehensive analysis of the NRA's political spending is inherently incomplete. The NRA uses its "Institute for Legislative Action" [ILA] to do most of its political spending. The ILA is an arm of the NRA that keeps its donors secret. About $34 million of the $54 million that the NRA reported to the Federal Election Commission in the 2016 cycle – more than 60% of its total – came through the ILA.[30]

Second, some campaign spending often goes unreported because our laws have not kept pace with how groups use changing technology to influence elections. As McClatchy reported in 2016, "two people with close connections to the powerful gun lobby said its total election spending [during the 2016 cycle] actually approached or exceeded $70 million [far more than the $54 million reported to the FEC]. The reporting gap could be explained by the fact that independent groups are not required to reveal how much they spend on [certain] Internet or field operations, including get-out-the-vote efforts."[31]

There is also the matter of foreign interference in our elections. The FBI is investigating whether Russian nationals who are close to the Kremlin "funneled money to the National Rifle Association to help Donald Trump win the election," according to McClatchy.[32] Moreover, "a prominent Kremlin-linked Russian politician has methodically cultivated ties with leaders of the National Rifle Association and documented efforts in real time over six years to leverage those connections and gain deeper access into American politics," according to NPR.[33]

NRA'S LOBBYING SPENDING

Lobbying is another strategy that the NRA uses to accomplish its political goals. It is a prolific spender on Capitol Hill.

In recent years, the NRA has increased its federal lobbying spending dramatically, going from $1,815,000 in 2007 to $5,122,000 in 2017 — more than a 182% increase.

Its federal lobbying has secured votes on some of its priorities – and blocked bills that it opposes.

Since Congress passed an assault weapons ban in 1994, which it allowed to expire in 2004, not much substantive gun legislation has been signed into law. One exception is the "Protection of Lawful Commerce in Arms Act;" President George W. Bush signed it in 2005. The law shields corporations which manufacture and sell weapons from liability when their products harm people. The NRA called this legislation a "vitally important first step toward ending the anti-gun lobby's shameless attempts to bankrupt the American firearms industry."[34]

Other gun measures have all failed. The House and Senate have voted on proposals to close the "gun show loophole" to require purchasers at gun shows to undergo background checks and three-day waiting periods. None have gone to the president's desk.

Other NRA priorities have gained momentum. In 2017, the House of Representatives passed the "Concealed Carry Reciprocity Act" to permit concealed handguns across state lines. It awaits action in the Senate. The NRA has pushed this proposal as one of its priority bills.

The NRA's legislative advocacy is not limited to gun-related legislation, however. It has also been a stalwart opponent of the DISCLOSE Act, legislation that would shine a light on secret money in politics, including the money that is flowing through its Institute for Legislative Action, as discussed above. In 2017 – a year after it spent $33 million from secret sources influencing the 2016 election – the NRA listed the DISCLOSE Act as one of the bills it paid its lobbyists to defeat. The DISCLOSE Act is one of the bills that the NRA lists most frequently on its lobbying reports.

NRA TIES TO THE AMERICAN LEGISLATIVE EXCHANGE COUNCIL (ALEC)

Much of the NRA's work occurs at the state level, where it has used the American Legislative Exchange Council (ALEC) to pursue its policy agenda. One of the most notorious laws that the NRA has pushed for the past decade is known as "stand your ground."

ALEC brings state legislators and corporate lobbyists together behind closed doors to draft and plot the passage of "model legislation" that furthers the corporate interests of its members.[35] ALEC's state legislative members take the model bills and introduce them in state legislatures throughout the country. ALEC staff offers state legislators talking points, boilerplate press releases, and other support to help push the bills over the finish line. ALEC describes itself as a charity, but Common Cause has filed a whistleblower complaint with the Internal Revenue Service challenging its charitable tax status, which gives ALEC's corporate donors a tax write-off for their support of the work that ALEC does to influence corporate-backed legislation.

In 2005, Florida adopted a "stand your ground" law that grants individuals a right to use deadly force, without any duty to retreat, if they reasonably believe it is necessary to "prevent death or great bodily harm . . . or to prevent he commission of a forcible felony."[36] Put another way, "stand your ground" is a "self-defense doctrine essentially permitting anyone feeling threatened in a confrontation to shoot their way out," according to Mother Jones.[37]

After Florida passed "stand your ground," the NRA's then-Executive Vice President Wayne LaPierre said it was "the first step of a multi-state strategy. There's a big tailwind we have, moving from state legislature to state legislature."[38]

With ALEC's help, the tailwind was felt across the country. An NRA lobbyist took the Florida law and worked with ALEC members on ALEC's "Criminal Justice Task Force" to draft model "stand your ground" legislation that passed in various forms[39] in at least 24 states.[40]

Florida's law was at issue in the nationally publicized trial of George Zimmerman, who was acquitted on self-defense grounds after killing Trayvon Martin, an unarmed Black teenager, in 2012.

SOLUTIONS TO REBALANCE OUR DEMOCRACY

Americans continue to organize to advance policies that will safeguard our communities from the crisis of gun violence. With every surge in the shocking violence affecting our towns, neighborhoods, and schools, people renew their pushes for changes to the laws that regulate how guns are bought, sold, and handled.

Despite the public support they enjoy, most of these proposals stall. People often cite the NRA's political contributions as a major reason for the ongoing stalemate. And as this report has detailed, the NRA's organizing power and political spending are significant. Too many politicians are beholden to the NRA and fear its influence in their election.

That's where voters come in.

Our democracy should be of, by, and for the people. We need to restore balance to our elections, and ensure everyone has an equal voice and equal say in the decisions that affect our lives – including laws that protect our schools, our homes, and our communities from gun violence.

Working together, we can strengthen our democracy to make our leaders more responsive to their real bosses – we the people. Here are five concrete solutions to shift power away from special interests like the NRA and empower the rest of us. There is more we must do – but here are places we can start to make our democracy more accountable and reflective.

1. Register and vote! Voting is the most important tool we have as citizens to hold our elected officials accountable. Our votes make us all equal and more powerful than we realize – but only if we show

up and cast them. In many jurisdictions, you can register to vote online. Other places may require you to mail in a voter registration form or bring it to your local elections office. In many states, young people can "pre-register" to vote before they turn 18. You can find out how to register in your state by going to http://www.vote.org/. If you have problems registering or any questions about voting, including what sort of identification you may need to bring to the polls, the rules for early voting, and the location of your polling place, you can call a nonpartisan Election Protection hotline run by the Election Protection Coalition. The phone number is 866-OUR-VOTE; you also can visit the Election Protection coalition online at www.866OurVote.org.

2. Urge your state to implement policies to modernize how Americans can participate in the voting process. Policies include pre-registration for 16- and 17-year olds, automatic voter registration, and early voting. Every eligible American has a right to vote and the process should reflect the way we live and work in the 21st century. Voting should be convenient, secure, fair, and accessible for all Americans. That means passing and implementing innovative policies to streamline the registration process and modernize election administration.

- Automatic voter registration will help modernize the out-of-date voter registration systems and databases in most states. Automatically registering eligible voters when they do business with Departments of Motor Vehicles and other government agencies will streamline our systems. Nine states and the District of Columbia have approved automatic voter registration, and momentum is building to pass this common-sense reform in other jurisdictions. As this policy is implemented, it has the potential to add tens of millions of voters to the voter rolls.

- Pre-registration for 16- and 17-year olds lets young people sign-up to vote so that they can make their voices heard in the first election in which they are eligible to participate. Sixteen states and the District of Columbia have this policy in place.

- Early voting helps ensure that voting is fair and accessible. Americans should have some flexibility when it comes to casting their ballots. Most states allow some form of early voting during a set-period of time before the election. This ensures that Americans who work or may be traveling on Election Day can cast their ballots. Still, 13 states do not permit early voting and require a specific excuse to vote absentee. Learn more about your state's procedures by visiting the nonpartisan Election Protection website, www.866OurVote.org.

3. Change the way we pay for political campaigns to empower all Americans, not just the wealthy few. This means boosting the role of small dollar donors in our elections. With each election cycle, our elected leaders depend on larger and larger contributions from a smaller and smaller share of our population. As a result, our leaders listen more to a handful of deep-pocketed donors and interests than to everyday Americans. To ensure that everyone has a real voice in politics, we need policies that put small dollar donors at the center of campaign finance, using matching public funds, tax credits, or small-dollar vouchers to encourage and supplement their giving. Providing public funding support to amplify the role of ordinary Americans in financing elections also allows more people to run for office – helping elect officeholders more reflective of the community at large – and allows candidates to spend more time listening to their constituents, and leads to policies more responsive to public needs and less skewed by wealthy interests. Connecticut has one of the most effective voluntary citizen-funded election systems in our country, with more than 75% of successful candidates participating in the program. Unlike Congress, Connecticut's leg-

islature passed major changes to its gun laws in the wake of the
Sandy Hook Elementary School shooting.[41] The state prohibited
more than 100 types of assault weapons, gun magazines with capacity of more than 10 rounds, and expanded background checks,
among other changes to its laws. Large municipalities throughout
the country are adopting these programs.

4. Shine a light on secret money in politics. A strong, 21st century democracy requires strong transparency and disclosure laws so that
everyone knows who is funding political campaigns. Secret money
in elections is unacceptable and undemocratic. More than $800 mil-
lion from secret sources has infected our elections at the federal
level alone since Citizens United in 2010. As described above, the
bulk of the NRA's spending in recent years has come with very
limited disclosure – and it has fought hard to keep it that way by
lobbying against the DISCLOSE Act in Congress. Still, states like
California, Connecticut, Maryland, Massachusetts, Montana, New
Mexico, and Rhode Island are leading the way with enhanced disclosure laws for state elections.

5. Create #FairMaps and end gerrymandering. Democracy should
mean that everyone counts and has fair and equal representation.
Voters should pick their elected representatives, rather than having
politicians pick their constituents. Building off several legal victories
and successes in creating strong systems in California and Arizona,
efforts to implement solutions that increase fairness and transparency in drawing political boundaries are moving across the country. Redistricting that puts people first requires several elements.
Every person living in a community must be fully and accurately
counted. This can be achieved through improved census outreach
and data collection while ending prison gerrymandering, the counting of prisoners where the prison is located instead of where they
previously lived. Districts must adhere to the requirements of the
Voting Rights Act and decision-makers should prioritize keeping

communities of interest together. A transparent process that allows the public to fully engage requires meetings of decision-makers to be held in public, enforces strong conflict of interest protections, and makes data and software being used to draw districts publicly available. No deliberations among decision-makers should be kept from the people through legislative privilege or other means.

Of course, none of these solutions alone will solve all our problems. But they will help to elevate the power of everyday Americans.

To learn more about these solutions, and to sign-up for action alerts nationally and in your state, sign-up at www.commoncause.org and get ready to plug-in and participate.

11

Walmart's C.E.O. Steps Into the Gun Debate. Other C.E.O.s Should Follow.

BY ANDREW ROSS SORKIN

Midday Tuesday Doug McMillon, Walmart's chief executive, sent me a surprise email. He shared a series of policies the company was about to make public about combating gun violence since the mass shooting that killed 22 people at one of his El Paso stores last month.

Mr. McMillon's email was a reply of sorts to an open letter I had written to him, along with the outcry he heard from scores of Americans, calling on him to use his leverage as the leader of the country's largest retailer to create a model for more responsible gun-selling practices.

Under Mr. McMillon, Walmart already had stopped selling assault-style guns and raised the age requirement for all gun buyers to 21. But five years into his tenure as chief executive of a company based in Arkansas that reaches into virtually every corner of the country, he had been reluctant to speak publicly against gun violence, fearing a political and customer backlash. Yet he forcefully entered the debate on Tuesday.

In his own open letter to Walmart employees, Mr. McMillon, a boyish-looking 52-year-old from Jonesboro, Ark., with a measured disposition, said the company would stop selling ammunition used for handguns and military-style weapons, completely end the sale of handguns and discourage anyone from carrying weapons in his stores (even in "open carry" states).

In a series of letters to congressional leaders and President Trump, Mr. McMillon called for a debate about reauthorizing the assault-weapons ban and to finance research on gun violence.

Mr. McMillon's move could prove to be a watershed.

His decision to engage in a meaningful conversation about responsible gun sales in America could give license to other business leaders to enter the conversation.

Until now, many top executives in corporate America — with some notable exceptions — refused to acknowledge the roles they could play in curbing the epidemic of gun violence. They invariably pointed to politicians in Washington as the ones who were responsible for solving the crisis.

For example, Al Kelly, the chief executive of Visa, whose network has been used repeatedly to carry out mass murders, has ducked any attempt to even discuss what his company could do to help. Mr. Kelly likes to say, as he did earlier this summer, "We are in the business of facilitating legal commerce. That's what we do. Our job is not to set or interpret, but to follow the law."

Mr. Kelly and other chief executives might want to study Mr. McMillon's example. He has chosen not to sell certain products even though they are legal.

"It's clear to us that the status quo is unacceptable," Mr. McMillon wrote to employees.

Years ago Walmart imposed age limits and background checks on gun sales that go beyond federal law. For example, the company requires a "green light" on a background check — meaning that it receives an affirmative go-ahead from the government — but federal law allows retailers to sell the weapon if the background check has not been returned by the government within three business days. Walmart also videotapes the sale at the register, which is also not required by federal law. And Mr. McMillon's new policy of discouraging customers' open carrying of weapons in his stores, even when the applicable state law allows for it, is a demonstration for business leaders that common sense can prevail.

Mr. McMillon said he wanted to share the company's processes with other retailers. "We are exploring ways to share the technical specifications and compliance controls for our proprietary firearms sales technology platform," he wrote. "This system navigates the tens of millions of possible combinations of federal, state and local laws, regulations and licensing requirements that come into effect based on where the firearm is being sold and who is purchasing it."

Critics will argue that Mr. McMillon isn't going far enough, and it is true that he could have gone further, for example by endorsing a ban on assault weapons rather than simply calling for a congressional debate. Another argument is that Walmart should stop selling guns altogether.

But discontinuing all gun sales would only undermine the company's role in helping develop more responsible processes throughout the industry. My open letter to him suggested he continue to sell some guns because it would give him leverage over the system in a way that would be impossible otherwise.

Prominent gun control advocates like former Representative Gabrielle Giffords congratulated Mr. McMillon.

"Walmart's action is another sign that the private sector has had enough with America's gun violence crisis," she said in a statement.

"Addressing a problem this big requires leaders from across American society to be part of the solution. Walmart's announcement should be applauded by all Americans, and I'm hopeful it will inspire elected leaders to follow in their footsteps."

Hopefully the inspiration isn't confined to politicians — or to Mr. McMillon. Which C.E.O. will be next?

12

Time to Bring Federal Domestic Violence Gun Laws in Line with Today's Reality

BY SHANNON WATTS, *Founder, Moms
Demand Action* **AND SARAH BURD-SHARPS,**
Director of Research, Everytown for Gun Safety

When abusive partners have access to a gun the toll of domestic violence on the lives of women is tragic—roughly one woman is shot to death by an intimate partner in the United States every 10 hours.[1] Yet that is only part of the story.

Guns are used by abusive partners to control, coerce, and injure, to threaten children and indeed to terrorize whole communities. An Everytown analysis revealed that in more than half of mass shootings over the past decade, the perpetrator shot a current or former intimate partner or family member during the incident.[2] And about one-third of mass shooters had a history of domestic violence.[3] The presence of a gun in a domestic violence situation makes it five times more likely that an abusive partner will kill his female victim.[4] The ripple effects of firearms in the hands of an abusive partner extend far beyond that one relationship, deeply impacting the lives of the children who witness or live with the abuse and the relatives, colleagues, and law enforcement officers who respond to it.

We have come far in our understanding of how to protect women from violent abusive partners. Over the past 25 years, there has been bipartisan support for laws limiting access to guns for the most dangerous domestic offenders in order to protect women, survivors of abuse, and their communities. But the protection offered by existing federal laws is a highly imperfect patchwork sorely in need of an update. Research has pointed to policy solutions that would pay big dividends in terms of lives saved and injuries avoided. And individual states are already acting on this knowledge. It's past time for Congress to take action to protect women across the nation.

What holes in our patchwork of federal gun laws must be filled to bring greater safety to our communities?

TIME TO UPDATE THE DEFINITION OF AN INTIMATE PARTNER

In the mid '90s, when key laws protecting women from violent abusers with guns were enacted, American women were far more likely to get married and to have children, than they are today. They were also likely to marry earlier. Fast forward to 2020 and relationship trends have changed but those same definitions from decades ago still shape the laws we rely on nationally and in many states to prevent abusive partners from using guns to injure their intimate partners—or worse.

Federal laws that prohibit a domestic abuser from purchasing a firearm apply to all of the traditional relationships above. But the laws don't cover abusive dating relationships, including romantic and intimate partners who have not lived together and do not have a child together. In these cases, by current federal law, a dating partner is not only allowed to keep any firearms they already have after a misdemeanor assault conviction, but can also buy more guns. So rather than improving our ability to safeguard women's lives over time, the proportion of the population protected by federal law is shrinking as more women choose to marry later, if at all. Today, more women are killed by their boyfriends and dating partners than by their spouses.[5] It's way past time to change the law to keep up with changes in our society. It's time to close this gap—commonly referred to as the "boyfriend loophole."

TIME TO UPDATE THE BACKGROUND CHECK SYSTEM TO APPLY TO ALL GUN SALES.

It is well known among people convicted of domestic violence crimes that they can easily acquire a gun from an unlicensed private gun seller because these unlicensed sellers, whether online or at a gun show, are exempt from the federal background check requirement. In 2018 alone, there were nearly 1.2 million ads posted for firearm sales where no background check was legally required, according to an Everytown investigation of the online gun marketplace Armslist.com. One in 9 prospective online buyers on Armslist.com would have failed a background check at a licensed dealer.[6]

Our current national system for screening people for disqualification from having a firearm was created in 1994. But a lot has changed in the over a quarter of a century since then, including the growth of a thriving online market of websites that enable private, unlicensed individuals to easily sell guns to other private purchasers. Twenty-two states and Washington, DC, have, at least in part, closed this loophole with laws signed by governors from both parties.[7] But some of these state laws only apply to handguns, leaving 28 states that allow alternative options. It is time to close this dangerous loophole in the federal background check system.

TIME TO RECOGNIZE STALKING IN THE CYCLE OF INTIMATE PARTNER VIOLENCE

The evidence of the relationship between stalking and intimate partner homicide against women is mounting—most intimate partner homicide is preceded by stalking shortly before the attack.[8] In a 2018 survey of victim calls to the National Domestic Violence Hotline, 3 in 4 people who reported being threatened with a gun had also been stalked by their partner.[9] Stalking is recognized as a predictor of lethality in intimate partner relationships. And yet federal law allows men convicted of misdemeanor stalking to buy and possess guns and does not require stalkers to surrender the guns they already have. It's not hard to imagine that stalking, especially cyber-stalking, has increased dramatically with our 24/7 use of social media, GPS, and the wide array of new technologies that enable abusive partners to harass, threaten, and track their partners' every move using technology. Again, it's time to bring our federal laws into the world we live in today and to prevent all convicted stalkers from accessing guns.

TIME TO PROHIBIT FIREARMS EARLIER IN THE CYCLE OF DOMESTIC ABUSE

While federal law prohibits those under a final domestic violence protective order from buying or having guns, it does not prohibit those subject to temporary domestic violence restraining orders, also called ex parte orders, from purchasing or accessing firearms. Those temporary orders are often the first legal step taken by a survivor in a domestic violence situation—after many other strategies have failed. As such, they are a time of potentially acute vulnerability, with grave possibilities of harm, and a serious need for protection. While we must ensure people under these orders have ready access to the courts, we must prohibit them from having guns while the orders are in place.

Ten states have taken action to prohibit people under a temporary order from possessing guns. And researchers compared the states with and without this firearm restriction and found considerable life-saving advantages to prohibiting gun access during this emergency period. States with the restriction saw a 16 percent decrease in intimate partner homicide with a firearm.[10] Failure to close this gap can be lethal.

The damage that domestic violence does to the lives of women and their families is part of the public conversation. But far less recognized is the fact that domestic violence is, to a significant degree, a gun violence problem. Nearly 60 percent of women murdered by an intimate partner are killed with a gun. In 2018, the lives of 679 women were cut short by intimate partner gun homicide.[11]

The goal in closing these loopholes once and for all is simple— protect our sisters, mothers, and daughters by preventing those who already have taken dangerous actions against their intimate partner from buying or getting access to a gun. Because this gun can facilitate the path from abuse to intimidation to injury and even death.

The good news is: We know that common-sense gun laws to keep guns out of the hands of domestic abusers work. In the case of dating partners, research shows that when states broadened laws beyond the existing federal firearm prohibition laws to cover abusive dating partners, states experienced a 16 percent reduction in intimate partner firearm homicide rates. States where temporary domestic violence restraining orders were included as a disqualifying factor also experienced a 16 percent decrease.[12]

What's next? Everytown for Gun Safety strongly supports these proposed bills that would bring our laws in line with today's reality in each of these areas:

- Violence Against Women Reauthorization Act of 2019 (H.R. 1585 / S. 2843), which would prohibit dating partners, stalkers, and people under temporary domestic violence restraining orders from having guns.[13]

- Bipartisan Background Checks Act of 2019 (H.R. 8) & the Background Check Expansion Act (S. 42), which would require background checks on all gun sales, including gun shows and online sales.[14]

- Zero Tolerance for Domestic Abusers Act of 2019 (H.R. 569) & the Protecting Domestic Violence and Stalking Victims Act of 2019 (S. 120), which would prohibit dating partners and stalkers from having guns.[15]

Imagine if our current pornography laws didn't factor in the impact of the internet. Or if child custody laws were silent on the rights and responsibilities of unmarried parents. The ability of those laws to protect vulnerable populations would be severely hampered. So, too, are our current federal firearms laws with respect to the protection of women. We are taking on twenty-first century challenges with twentieth century tools, and losing precious women's lives to intimate partner gun homicide twice a day. Every day.

As the mothers of six daughters between the two of us, we are hopeful our federal legislators will work to save women's lives and increase public safety through these proven legislative updates.

13

Local Laws and Local Enforcement Are Critical to Halt Gun Violence Between Intimate Partners

RACHEL GRABER, Director of Public Policy
at the National Coalition Against Domestic Violence
AND ROBERTA VALENTE, Policy Consultant
at the National Coalition Against Domestic Violence

"Time to Bring Federal Domestic Violence Gun Laws in Line with Today's Reality" outlined a number of recommendations for changes to federal law to keep firearms out of the hands of adjudicated domestic and dating abusers and stalkers. In addition to these important updates, there are other, smaller legislative changes Congress should make to existing law in order to keep guns out of the hands of domestic abusers. States should also pass laws to address abusers' firearm access, and local agencies should take measures to enforce these laws. The three levels of government—federal, state, and local—have complementary and sometimes intertwining roles to play to disarm abusers.

Recommended improvements federal law fall into two categories—a technical fix to the federal law described in "Armed Abusers" and tools to improve enforcement of existing laws at the state and local level. The technical fix is the simple addition of four words to the federal law prohibiting domestic violence misdemeanants from possessing firearms. The text of the law defines a misdemeanor crime of domestic violence in part as a "misdemeanor under Federal, State, or Tribal law."[1] Although the Department of Justice has long interpreted "State" as including jurisdictions therein,[2] an outlying decisions by the 10th[3] Federal Circuit Court means that in most of the country, domestic violence misdemeanants convicted under local laws are prohibited from possessing firearms under federal law. However, in the geographic area covered by the 10th Federal Circuit Court, people convicted of domestic violence under local laws are allowed to have firearms. This gap can be closed with the simple clarifying addition of the term "municipal" to the definition of the misdemeanor crime of domestic violence.

The remaining recommendations for changes to federal law primarily center around providing information and resources to state and local governments and law enforcement agencies so they can better enforce existing laws. This includes, for example, giving local governments the flexibility to use federal grant dollars through the Violence Against Women Act to develop and implement policies and protocols to ensure adjudicated abusers relinquish their firearms upon becoming prohibited. It also means sharing information with local law enforcement when a prohibited abuser tries to purchase a gun and fails a background check or, in some cases, fails a background check after already having taken possession of a firearm. The federal government can also boost local capacity and prosecutorial options by cross-deputizing local prosecutors and law enforcement agents as Special Assistant United States Attorneys and ATF agents respectively.

States have an important role to play in addressing abusers' access to firearms. Although the federal government prohibits certain adjudicated abusers from possessing firearms, states should also have their own laws restricting firearm possession for adjudicated abusers. The structure of governance in the United States is such that federal law enforcement agencies, prosecutors, and courts enforce federal law, and state law enforcement agencies, prosecutors, and courts enforce state laws. Most domestic violence cases are adjudicated at the state level, and states cannot prosecute abusers for violations of federal law. Thus, it is important that state law restricts abusers' firearm access.

States should also enact stricter laws than what is currently in federal statute. Not only should abusive current and former spouses, current and former cohabitants, and abusers who share a child in common with the victim be prohibited from purchasing or possessing firearms, this restriction should also apply to adjudicated dating partners. Similar to the recommendations in Chapter 12, state laws prohibiting the purchase and possession of firearms should apply not only to domestic violence misdemeanants and respondents to final protective orders but also to respondents to ex parte protective orders and stalking misdemeanants.

Because enforcement of domestic violence laws primarily happens at the state level, state laws can also address what happens to an adjudicated abuser's existing guns once the individual is prohibited from possessing them. Many states have a statutory procedure as to how a prohibited person must dispose of their firearms, to whom they can transfer the firearms, how they prove to the court that they are no longer in possession of firearms, and what they need to do to regain control of their firearms at such a time as they are no longer prohibited from possessing them. States should pass laws requiring adjudicated abusers to relinquish their firearms and setting out a process for relinquishment, and local jurisdictions should develop and implement policies and protocols to ensure the safe relinquishment, recovery, storage, and, at such a time as the person is no longer prohibited, return of firearms. For more information about state domestic violence and firearms laws, see disarmdv.org.

Legislative solutions to disarming domestic abusers cannot rest solely with the federal government. Every level of government has a role to play. Strengthening and enforcing these laws will save lives.

14

Extreme Risk Laws Save Lives

BY ROBYN THOMAS, *Executive Director*
of Giffords Law Center

In April 2018, a woman in Broward County, Florida, received a series of alarming texts from her husband. Her husband, who organized music functions at schools, threatened to kill her and wrote that an upcoming event was "just a big ploy to get all these people there so I can just [expletive] kill them all."[1]

The man, who had begun displaying increasingly erratic behavior after starting chemotherapy, had already been the subject of a call to law enforcement when he started screaming and yelling to his brother that he was going to shoot himself and the police.

Fortunately, law enforcement in Broward County had a new tool at their disposal that enabled them to take swift action to protect their community. Thanks to Florida's extreme risk law, enacted in March 2018 in response to the Parkland massacre, law enforcement officers were able to petition for an extreme risk protection order (ERPO) to prevent the man from purchasing guns for one year.

With nearly 38,000 lives lost to gun violence each year and tens of thousands more Americans injured, the scope of our nation's gun violence crisis is daunting. It's understandable to feel intimidated, even prematurely defeated, by a number that large, to assume that this uniquely American epidemic is the immutable byproduct of a dangerous decision our country made to inextricably intertwine freedom and firearms.

The gun lobby wants you to believe that these many thousands of gun deaths and injuries are simply the cost of doing business, but this couldn't be farther from the truth. Gun violence, in fact, *is* preventable. As executive director of Giffords Law Center for the past 14 years, I've spent the majority of my career fighting for the laws, policies, and programs proven to save lives from gun violence. What the gun lobby doesn't want you to know is that gun laws actually do work.

Every year, our *Annual Gun Law Scorecard* demonstrates that states with the strongest gun laws tend to have the lowest gun death rates.[2] California, where Giffords Law Center was founded over 25 years ago after a mass shooting at a law firm, is a prime example of how state-level progress can save lives. Our state, which today has some of the strongest gun laws in the nation, has cut its gun death rate in half over the past 25 years.[3]

Across the country each day, gun violence unfolds in myriad tragic and disparate ways. Two-thirds of gun deaths are suicides. Most other gun deaths are homicides, many connected to retaliatory violence, but others related to domestic violence and mass shootings.

There is no single solution that will end our country's gun violence epidemic, no one law or policy or program that will put a stop to the heartbreak and trauma that far too many American families suffer every year. What we need instead—what we at Giffords Law Center and our allies in the gun violence prevention movement have been working painstakingly, for decades, to assemble—is a suite of tools that will work in concert to chip away at the problem.

We need universal background checks, and safe storage, and community violence intervention programs, and regulation of assault weapons and ghost guns. We also need extreme risk laws, which enable those best positioned to notice warning signs to take action.

Gun violence usually doesn't happen out of the blue—in the case of mass shootings in particular, warning signs often abound. According to an FBI study of the pre-attack behaviors of active shooters, each perpetrator displayed an average of four to five concerning behaviors.[4]

The Parkland school shooter was the subject of multiple tips to the FBI and calls to law enforcement, yet because he didn't fall into any of the categories that would prohibit him from purchasing or owning firearms—like a previous felony conviction or involuntary mental health commitment—he was able to legally purchase the AR-15-style rifle he used to murder 17 of his classmates and teachers.[5] Similarly, the parents of the perpetrator of the 2014 Isla Vista shooting contacted the police over their concerns about their son's violent behaviors and concerning YouTube videos, but deputies determined he didn't meet the criteria for an involuntary hold and he went on to kill six people.[6]

Suicide, often the byproduct of serious depression or other types of mental illness, is also frequently preceded by warning signs.[7] Firearms are the most lethal of the commonly available means of suicide in the US: 85% of suicide attempts with a gun end in death, while less than 5% of non-firearm suicide attempts result in death.[8] The hopeful truth is that suicide, much like other forms of gun violence, is preventable: 90% of individuals who survive a suicide attempt do not go on to die by suicide.[9] By taking action in the face of warning signs, we can prevent harm and save lives.

This is exactly what extreme risk laws do: empower individuals to take action when they see warning signs. In 19 states and the District of Columbia, law enforcement—and in some states, family members—can petition the court for a temporary order restricting access to guns when a person poses a demonstrated risk to themselves or others. After the tragedy in Parkland, these laws spread across the country, with eight states passing extreme risk laws in 2018 and four states plus the District of Columbia passing them in 2019. In 2020, New Mexico and Virginia became the 18th and 19th states to enact extreme risk laws.[10]

In Florida, as in many other states, the judge first issues an emergency, or *ex parte* order, which lasts for up to 14 days. Before the *ex parte* order expires, there is a full hearing in which the respondent has the opportunity to contest the order. If the judge decides there is sufficient evidence to grant a final order, the petitioner must surrender any guns they own and is prohibited from purchasing any new firearms for the duration of the order, which lasts for up to one year unless extended by a judge.

Extreme risk laws have already been proven to save lives. In Connecticut and Indiana, studies have demonstrated that approximately one life was saved through an averted suicide for every 10 to 20 firearm removals.[11] These laws have not only been proven effective—they're broadly supported. According to a 2019 survey, 76% of Americans support a policy that would authorize law enforcement officers to temporarily remove guns from people who pose an immediate threat to themselves or others.[12]

Yet unsurprisingly, the NRA and other gun lobby groups have whipped themselves into a frenzy over extreme risk laws. For decades, the gun lobby has fervently opposed a wide range of evidence-based gun laws, from universal background checks to closing loopholes that allow abusive dating partners and stalkers to purchase guns.

Most recently, the NRA has spread false information about how extreme risk laws are the latest iteration of an elaborate plot to confiscate guns from law-abiding citizens. In response to this reckless and profit-driven fear-mongering, a "Second Amendment sanctuary" movement has sprung up in counties around the nation, fueled by sheriffs who mistakenly believe that they possess the singular authority to decide whether or not lawfully enacted gun regulations laws are constitutional.

Local officials who refuse to enforce gun laws passed by state legislatures are needlessly endangering the lives of their constituents. To make matters worse, many of the counties that have declared themselves "Second Amendment sanctuaries" have firearm suicide rates far higher than the national average.[13] These Americans—all Americans—deserve to be protected by these critical and lifesaving laws. Elected officials shouldn't be more concerned with protecting guns than protecting the lives of the people they're supposed to represent.

Last year, Giffords Law Center set out to better understand how these laws were working in practice. Our research team traveled to Florida to collect thousands of pages of case files for all ERPOs filed in the first year of law's existence, and spoke with key stakeholders responsible for implementing the law.

This February we released a report, *Preventing the Next Parkland: A Case Study of the Use and Implementation of Florida's Extreme Risk Law in Broward County*, documenting over 200 instances of threatened violence in Broward County in which law enforcement effectively used the state's new extreme risk law to intervene. Not only was this law used to disarm the man who texted his wife threatening a school shooting, it was also used to disarm a teenager struggling with depression who took a gun from his father's safe; a man who decapitated and beat ducklings before threatening to shoot his arresting officers; and a woman who told her friend that she would commit a "bloodbath" before killing herself.[14]

Judges in Broward County granted final orders in 87% of the cases that came before them. Firearms were seized in more than half of the cases, totaling 412 guns, an average of three per seizure. One individual surrendered 67 guns.[15]

Despite the gun lobby's best efforts, Florida sheriffs and law enforcement officers have spoken up in defense of the state's extreme risk law: Pinellas County Sheriff Bob Gualtieri has said that the extreme risk law created a much-needed tool for law enforcement, and indicated that "there's no doubt [the orders] have an impact and have prevented people from engaging in bad acts."[16] Polk County Sheriff Grady Judd, a self-described "huge Second Amendment person" endorsed ERPOs as creating an important, temporary cooling-off period to defuse significant dangers.[17] In an interview, Captain Michael Riggio of the Broward County Sheriff's Office Threat Management Division said this tool helped him and his officers "prevent serious harm from occurring in the community" while effectively balancing due process and gun rights concerns.[18]

In addition to exploring Broward County's use of the law, our report made recommendations for legislators, law enforcement, and courts tasked with enacting and implementing these laws. First and most importantly, we recommended that every state pass some version of an extreme risk law. Our best practice recommendations for implementation include, among others, allowing family members— often the first to notice warning signs—to petition for ERPOs in every state; requiring law enforcement to develop local protocols and train officers on ERPOs; and ensuring compliance with firearm surrender, ideally to law enforcement or a licensed dealer.

Our report and other research have demonstrated the clear promise and potential of extreme risk laws to intervene in crises and prevent them from turning into tragedies, which is why we're calling on every state in the nation to enact these laws. We're calling on the states that have already passed extreme risk laws to make sure that these laws are broadly understood among law enforcement and court personnel, and that they're properly implemented and studied so that we can continue to improve on their effectiveness.

In moments of crisis, there's often no time to lose. If we're lucky, a small window of opportunity exists during which a concerned friend or family member notices signs of distress and can intervene before tragedy strikes. Let's make this chance count for something.

15

The Police Are Still Out of Control

BY FRANK SERPICO

In the opening scene of the 1973 movie "Serpico," I am shot in the face—or to be more accurate, the character of Frank Serpico, played by Al Pacino, is shot in the face. Even today it's very difficult for me to watch those scenes, which depict in a very realistic and terrifying way what actually happened to me on Feb. 3, 1971. I had recently been transferred to the Narcotics division of the New York City Police Department, and we were moving in on a drug dealer on the fourth floor of a walk-up tenement in a Hispanic section of Brooklyn. The police officer backing me up instructed me (since I spoke Spanish) to just get the apartment door open "and leave the rest to us."

One officer was standing to my left on the landing no more than eight feet away, with his gun drawn; the other officer was to my right rear on the stairwell, also with his gun drawn. When the door opened, I pushed my way in and snapped the chain. The suspect slammed the door closed on me, wedging in my head and right shoulder and arm. I couldn't move, but I aimed my snub-nose Smith & Wesson revolver at the perp (the movie version unfortunately goes a little Hollywood here, and has Pacino struggling and failing to raise a much-larger 9-millimeter automatic). From behind me no help came. At that moment my anger got the better of me. I made the almost fatal mistake of taking my eye off the perp and screaming to the officer on my left: "What the hell you waiting for? Give me a hand!" I turned back to face a gun blast in my face. I had cocked my weapon and fired back at him almost in the same instant, probably as reflex action, striking him. (He was later captured.)

When I regained consciousness, I was on my back in a pool of blood trying to assess the damage from the gunshot wound in my cheek. Was this a case of small entry, big exit, as often happens with bullets? Was the back of my head missing? I heard a voice saying, "Don' worry, you be all right, you be all right," and when I opened my eyes I saw an old Hispanic man looking down at me like Carlos Castaneda's Don Juan. My "backup" was nowhere in sight. They hadn't even called for assistance—I never heard the famed "Code 1013," meaning "Officer Down." They didn't call an ambulance either, I later learned; the old man did. One patrol car responded to investigate, and realizing I was a narcotics officer rushed me to a nearby hospital (one of the officers who drove me that night said, "If I knew it was him, I would have left him there to bleed to death," I learned later).

The next time I saw my "back-up" officers was when one of them came to the hospital to bring me my watch. I said, "What the hell am I going to do with a watch? What I needed was a back-up. Where were you?" He said, "Fuck you," and left. Both my "back-ups" were later awarded medals for saving my life.

I still don't know exactly what happened on that day. There was never any real investigation. But years later, Patrick Murphy, who was police commissioner at the time, was giving a speech at one of my alma maters, the John Jay College of Criminal Justice, and I confronted him. I said, "My name is Frank Serpico, and I've been carrying a bullet in my head for over 35 years, and you, Mr. Murphy, are the man I hold responsible. You were the man who was brought as commissioner to take up the cause that I began — rooting out corruption. You could have protected me; instead you put me in harm's way. What have you got to say?" He hung his head, and had no answer.

Even now, I do not know for certain why I was left trapped in that door by my fellow police officers. But the Narcotics division was rotten to the core, with many guys taking money from the very drug dealers they were supposed to bust. I had refused to take bribes and had testified against my fellow officers. Police make up a peculiar subculture in society. More often than not they have their own moral code of behavior, an "us against them" attitude, enforced by a Blue Wall of Silence. It's their version of the Mafia's omerta. Speak out, and you're no longer "one of us." You're one of "them." And as James Fyfe, a nationally recognized expert on the use of force, wrote in his 1993 book about this issue, *Above The Law*, officers who break the code sometimes won't be helped in emergency situations, as I wasn't.

Forty-odd years on, my story probably seems like ancient history to most people, layered over with Hollywood legend. For me it's not, since at the age of 78 I'm still deaf in one ear and I walk with a limp and I carry fragments of the bullet near my brain. I am also, all these years later, still persona non grata in the NYPD. Never mind that, thanks to Sidney Lumet's direction and Al Pacino's brilliant acting, "Serpico" ranks No. 40 on the American Film Institute's list of all-time movie heroes, or that as I travel around the country and the world, police officers often tell me they were inspired to join the force after seeing the movie at an early age.

In the NYPD that means little next to my 40-year-old heresy, as they see it. I still get hate mail from active and retired police officers. A couple of years ago after the death of David Durk — the police officer who was one of my few allies inside the department in my efforts to expose graft — the Internet message board "NYPD Rant" featured some choice messages directed at me. "Join your mentor, Rat scum!" said one. An ex-con recently related to me that a precinct captain had once said to him, "If it wasn't for that fuckin' Serpico, I coulda been a millionaire today." My informer went on to say, "Frank, you don't seem to understand, they had a well-oiled money making machine going and you came along and threw a handful of sand in the gears."

In 1971 I was awarded the Medal of Honor, the NYPD's highest award for bravery in action, but it wasn't for taking on an army of corrupt cops. It was most likely due to the insistence of Police Chief Sid Cooper, a rare good guy who was well aware of the murky side of the NYPD that I'd try to expose. But they handed the medal to me like an afterthought, like tossing me a pack of cigarettes. After all this time, I've never been given a proper certificate with my medal. And although living Medal of Honor winners are typically invited to yearly award ceremonies, I've only been invited once — and it was by Bernard Kerick, who ironically was the only NYPD commissioner to later serve time in prison. A few years ago, after the New York Police Museum refused my guns and other memorabilia, I loaned them to the Italian-American museum right down street from police headquarters, and they invited me to their annual dinner. I didn't know it was planned, but the chief of police from Rome, Italy, was there, and he gave me a plaque. The New York City police officers who were there wouldn't even look at me.

So my personal story didn't end with the movie, or with my retirement from the force in 1972. It continues right up to this day. And the reason I'm speaking out now is that, tragically, too little has really changed since the Knapp Commission, the outside investigative panel formed by then-Mayor John Lindsay after I failed at repeated internal efforts to get the police and district attorney to investigate rampant corruption in the force. Lindsay had acted only because finally, in desperation, I went to the New York Times, which put my story on the front page. Led by Whitman Knapp, a tenacious federal judge, the commission for at least a brief moment in time supplied what has always been needed in policing: outside accountability. As a result many officers were prosecuted and many more lost their jobs. But the commission disbanded in 1972 even though I had hoped (and had so testified) that it would be made permanent.

And today the Blue Wall of Silence endures in towns and cities across America. Whistleblowers in police departments — or as I like to call them, "lamp lighters," after Paul Revere — are still turned into permanent pariahs. The complaint I continue to hear is that when they try to bring injustice to light they are told by government officials: "We can't afford a scandal; it would undermine public confidence in our police." That confidence, I dare say, is already seriously undermined.

Things might have improved in some areas. The days when I served and you could get away with anything, when cops were better at accounting than at law enforcement — keeping meticulous records of the people they were shaking down, stealing drugs and money from dealers on a regular basis — all that no longer exists as systematically as it once did, though it certainly does in some places. Times have changed. It's harder to be a venal cop these days.

But an even more serious problem — police violence — has probably grown worse, and it's out of control for the same reason that graft once was: a lack of accountability.

I tried to be an honest cop in a force full of bribe-takers. But as I found out the hard way, police departments are useless at investigating themselves—and that's exactly the problem facing ordinary people across the country —including perhaps, Ferguson, Missouri, which has been a lightning rod for discontent even though the circumstances under which an African-American youth, Michael Brown, was shot remain unclear.

Today the combination of an excess of deadly force and near-total lack of accountability is more dangerous than ever: Most cops today can pull out their weapons and fire without fear that anything will happen to them, even if they shoot someone wrongfully. All a police officer has to say is that he believes his life was in danger, and he's typically absolved. What do you think that does to their psychology as they patrol the streets—this sense of invulnerability? The famous old saying still applies: Power corrupts, and absolute power corrupts absolutely. (And we still don't know how many of these incidents occur each year; even though Congress enacted the Violent Crime Control and Law Enforcement Act 20 years ago, requiring the Justice Department to produce an annual report on "the use of excessive force by law enforcement officers," the reports were never issued.)

It wasn't any surprise to me that, after Michael Brown was shot dead in Ferguson, officers instinctively lined up behind Darren Wilson, the cop who allegedly killed Brown. Officer Wilson may well have had cause to fire if Brown was attacking him, as some reports suggest, but it is also possible we will never know the full truth—whether, for example, it was really necessary for Wilson to shoot Brown at least six times, killing rather than just wounding him. As they always do, the police unions closed ranks also behind the officer in question. And the district attorney (who is often totally in bed with the police and needs their votes) and city power structure can almost always be counted on to stand behind the unions.

In some ways, matters have gotten even worse. The gulf between the police and the communities they serve has grown wider. Mind you, I don't want to say that police shouldn't protect themselves and have access to the best equipment. Police officers have the right to defend themselves with maximum force, in cases where, say, they are taking on a barricaded felon armed with an assault weapon. But when you are dealing every day with civilians walking the streets, and you bring in armored vehicles and automatic weapons, it's all out of proportion. It makes you feel like you're dealing with some kind of subversive enemy. The automatic weapons and bulletproof vest may protect the officer, but they also insulate him from the very society he's sworn to protect. All that firepower and armor puts an even greater wall between the police and society, and solidifies that "us-versus-them" feeling.

And with all due respect to today's police officers doing their jobs, they don't need all that stuff anyway. When I was cop I disarmed a man with three guns who had just killed someone. I was off duty and all I had was my snub-nose Smith & Wesson. I fired a warning shot, the guy ran off and I chased him down. Some police forces still maintain a high threshold for violence: I remember talking with a member of the Italian carabinieri, who are known for being very heavily armed. He took out his Beretta and showed me that it didn't even have a magazine inside. "You know, I got to be careful," he said. "Before I shoot somebody unjustifiably, I'm better off shooting myself." They have standards.

In the NYPD, it used to be you'd fire two shots and then you would assess the situation. You didn't go off like a madman and empty your magazine and reload. Today it seems these police officers just empty their guns and automatic weapons without thinking, in acts of callousness or racism. They act like they're in shooting galleries. Today's uncontrolled firepower, combined with a lack of good training and adequate screening of police academy candidates, has led to a devastating drop in standards. The infamous case of Amadou Diallo in New York—who was shot 41 times in 1999 for no obvious reason—is more typical than you might think. The shooters, of course, were absolved of any wrongdoing, as they almost always are. All a policeman has to say is that "the suspect turned toward me menacingly," and he does not have to worry about prosecution. In a 2010 case recorded on a police camera in Seattle, John Williams, a 50-year-old traditional carver of the Nuu-chah-nulth First Nations (tribes), was shot four times by police as he walked across the street with a pocketknife and a piece of cedar in his hands. He died at the scene. It's like the Keystone Kops, but without being funny at all.

Many white Americans, indoctrinated by the ridiculous number of buddy-cop films and police-themed TV shows that Hollywood has cranked out over the decades—almost all of them portraying police as heroes—may be surprised by the continuing outbursts of anger, the protests in the street against the police that they see in inner-city environments like Ferguson. But they often don't understand that these minority communities, in many cases, view the police as the enemy.

We want to believe that cops are good guys, but let's face it, any kid in the ghetto knows different. The poor and the disenfranchised in society don't believe those movies; they see themselves as the victims, and they often are.

Law enforcement agencies need to eliminate those who use and abuse the power of the law as they see fit. As I said to the Knapp Commission 43 years ago, we must create an atmosphere where the crooked cop fears the honest cop, and not the other way around. An honest cop should be able to speak out against unjust or illegal behavior by fellow officers without fear of ridicule or reprisals. Those that speak out should be rewarded and respected by their superiors, not punished.

We're not there yet.

It still strikes me as odd that I'm seen as a renegade cop and unwelcome by police in the city I grew up in. Because as far back as I can remember, all I wanted to be was a member of the NYPD. Even today, I love the police life. I love the work.

I grew up in Brooklyn, and shined shoes in my father's shop when I was a kid. My uncle was a member of the *carabinieri* in Italy, and when I was 13 my mother took me to see my only surviving grandparent, her father. So I met her brother the *carabinieri*, who was in civilian clothes but carried a Beretta sidearm. I just marveled at the respect and dignity with which he did his work, and how people respected him. My father, a World War I POW, also in his early years contemplated being a *carabinieri*, but he had his shoe-repair trade and became a craftsman. As a young boy I had no idea. All I knew was that I was impressed by my uncle's behavior. This guy could open doors.

It wasn't that I was completely naïve about what bad cops could be. As a boy of 8 or 9, returning home one evening after shining shoes on the parkway, I saw a white police officer savagely beating a frail black woman with his night stick as she lay prostrate on a parkway bench. She didn't utter a sound. All I could hear was the thud as the wood struck her skin and bones. (I was reminded of that 70-year-old incident recently when an Internet video showed a white police officer pummeling a black woman with his gloved fist in broad daylight — have police tactics really changed?)

But I also saw the good side of cops. I saw them standing on the running board of a car they had commandeered to chase a thief. When I was a few years older, and I wounded myself with a self-made zip gun, my mother took me to the hospital and two cops showed up, demanding, "Where's the gun?" I said I had no gun, that I'd just found a shell and when I tried to take the casing off, it exploded. They looked at me skeptically and asked me where I went to school. I said, "St. Francis Prep, and I want to be a cop just like you." They said, "If you don't smarten up you'll never make it that far." But they didn't give me a juvenile citation, as they could have. So I knew there were good cops out there.

I wasn't naive when I entered the force as a rookie patrolman on Sept. 11, 1959, either. I knew that some cops took traffic money, but I had no idea of the institutionalized graft, corruption and nepotism that existed and was condoned until one evening I was handed an envelope by another officer. I had no idea what was in it until I went to my car and found that it contained my share of the "nut," as it was called (a reference to squirrels hiding their nuts; some officers buried the money in jars buried in their backyards). Still, back then I was naive enough to believe that within the system there was someone who was not aware of what was going on and, once informed, would take immediate action to correct it.

I was wrong. The first place I went was to the mayor's department of investigation, where I was told outright I had a choice: 1) Force their hand, meaning I would be found face down in the East River; or 2) Forget about it. The rest you know, especially if you've seen the movie. After refusing to take money myself, but coming under relentless pressure to do so, I went successively to the inspector's office, the mayor's office and the district attorney. They each promised me action and didn't deliver. The lobbying power of the police was too strong. I discovered that I was all but alone in a world of institutionalized graft, where keeping the "pad" —all the money they skimmed—meant that officers spent more time tabulating their piece of the cake more than as guardians of the peace.

Over the years, politicians who wanted to make a difference didn't. They were too beholden to the police unions and the police vote. I wrote a letter to President Bill Clinton in 1994 addressing this very issue, saying that honest cops have never been rewarded, and maybe there ought to be a medal for them. He wrote back, but nothing changed. In New York City, then-Mayor Michael Bloomberg professed that things were going to change, but in the end he went right along with his commissioner, Ray Kelly, who was allowed to do whatever he wanted. Kelly had been a sergeant when I was on the force, and he'd known about the corruption, as did Murphy.

As for Barack Obama and his attorney general, Eric Holder, they gave speeches after Ferguson. But it's 20 years too late. It's the same old problem of political power talking, and it doesn't matter that both the president and his attorney general are African-American. Corruption is color blind. Money and power corrupt, and they are color blind too.

Only a few years ago, a cop who was in the same 81st Precinct I started in, Adrian Schoolcraft, was actually taken to a psych ward and handcuffed to a gurney for six days after he tried to complain about corruption—they wanted him to keep to a quota of summonses, and he wasn't complying. No one would have believed him except he hid a tape recorder in his room, and recorded them making their demands. Now he's like me, an outcast.

Every time I speak out on topics of police corruption and brutality, there are inevitably critics who say that I am out of touch and that I am old enough to be the grandfather of many of the cops who are currently on the force. But I've kept up the struggle, working with lamp lighters to provide them with encouragement and guidance; serving as an expert witness to describe the tactics that police bureaucracies use to wear them down psychologically; testifying in support of independent boards; developing educational guidance to young minority citizens on how to respond to police officers; working with the American Civil Liberties Union to expose the abuses of stun-gun technology in prisons; and lecturing in more high schools, colleges and reform schools than I can remember. A little over a decade ago, when I was a presenter at the Top Cops Award event hosted by TV host John Walsh, several police officers came up to me, hugged me and then whispered in my ear, "I gotta talk to you."

The sum total of all that experience can be encapsulated in a few simple rules for the future:

1. **Strengthen the selection process and psychological screening process for police recruits.** Police departments are simply a microcosm of the greater society. If your screening standards encourage corrupt and forceful tendencies, you will end up with a larger concentration of these types of individuals;

2. **Provide ongoing, examples-based training and simulations.** Not only telling but *showing* police officers how they are expected to behave and react is critical;

3. **Require community involvement from police officers** so they know the districts and the individuals they are policing. This will encourage empathy and understanding;

4. **Enforce the laws against everyone, including police officers.** When police officers do wrong, use those individuals as examples of what not to do—so that others know that this behavior will not be tolerated. And tell the police unions and detective endowment associations they need to keep their noses out of the justice system;

5. **Support the good guys.** Honest cops who tell the truth and behave in exemplary fashion should be honored, promoted and held up as strong positive examples of what it means to be a cop;

6. **Last but not least, police cannot police themselves.** Develop permanent, independent boards to review incidents of police corruption and brutality—and then fund them well and support them publicly. Only this can change a culture that has existed since the beginnings of the modern police department.

There are glimmers of hope that some of this is starting to happen, even in New York under Bill DeBlasio. In October 2014 DeBlasio's commissioner, Bill Bratton—who'd previously served a term as commissioner in New York as well as police chief in Los Angeles—made a crowd of police brass squirm in discomfort when he showed a hideous video montage of police officers mistreating members of the public and said he would "aggressively seek to get those out of the department who should not be here — the brutal, the corrupt, the racist, the incompetent." I found that very impressive.

And legislators are starting to act—and perhaps to free themselves of the political power of police. In Wisconsin, after being contacted by Mike Bell — a retired Air Force officer who flew in three wars and whose son was shot to death by police after being pulled over for a DUI – I'd like to believe I helped in a successful campaign to push through the nation's first law setting up outside review panels in cases of deaths in police custody.

Like the Knapp Commission in its time, they are just a start. But they are something.

NOTES

ARMED ABUSERS

1   Black, M.C., Basile, K.C., Breiding, M.J., Smith, S.G., Walters, M.L., Merrick, M.T., Chen, J. & Stevens, M. (2011). *The national intimate partner and sexual violence survey: 2010 summary report.* Retrieved from http://www.cdc.gov/violenceprevention/pdf/nisvs_report2010-a.pdf.

2   Ibid.

3   Catalano, S. (2015). Intimate partner violence, 1993–2010. *Bureau of Justice Statistics.* Retrieved from https://www.bjs.gov/content/pub/pdf/ipv9310.pdf.

4   Black, M.C., Basile, K.C., Breiding, M.J., Smith, S.G., Walters, M.L., Merrick, M.T., Chen, J. & Stevens, M. (2011). *The national intimate partner and sexual violence survey: 2010 summary report.* Retrieved from http://www.cdc.gov/violenceprevention/pdf/nisvs_report2010-a.pdf.

5   National Coalition Against Domestic Violence (n.d.). *Domestic violence.* Retrieved from https://assets.speakcdn.com/assets/2497/domestic_violence2.pdf.

6   Office of Representative Ayanna Pressley (2019, April 4). *Rep. Pressley pays tribute to her mother following the passage of VAWA* [Press release]. Retrieved from https://pressley.house.gov/media/press-releases/rep-pressley-s-pays-tribute-her-mother-following-passage-vawa.

7   Sorenson, S. B., & Schut, R. A. (2016). Nonfatal gun use in intimate partner violence: A systematic review of the literature. *Trauma, Violence, & Abuse.*

8   National Domestic Violence Hotline (2014). *Firearms and domestic violence.* Retrieved from http://www.thehotline.org/resources/firearms-dv/#tab-id-2.

9   National Domestic Violence Hotline (n.d.) *Firearms and domestic violence.* Retrieved from https://www.thehotline.org/resources/firearms-dv/.

10   McFarlane, J., Soeken. K., Campbell, J., Parker, B., Reel, S. & Silva, C. (1998). Severity of abuse to pregnant women and associated gun access of the perpetrator. *Public Health Nursing, 15*(3), 201–206. DOI: 10.1111/j.1525-1446.1998.tb00340.x_

11   Laing, K. (2016, June 23). Rep. Debbie Dingell gets personal in plea for gun vote. *The Detroit News. https://www.detroitnews.com/story/news/politics/2016/06/23/debbie-dingell-guns/86287562/*

12   Institute of Medicine (US) Committee on Women's Health Research (2010). *Women's health research: Progress, pitfalls, and promise.* National Academies Press.

13   Bridges, F. S., Tatum, K. M., & Kunselman, J. C. (2008). Domestic violence statutes and rates of intimate partner and family homicide: A research note. *Criminal Justice Policy Review, 19*(1), 117–130.

14   Violence Policy Center (2019). *When men murder women: An analysis of 2017 homicide data.* Retrieved from http://www.vpc.org/studies/wmmw2019.

15   Saltzman, L. E., Mercy, J. A., O'Carroll, P. W., Rosenberg, M. L., & Rhodes, P. H. (1992). Weapon involvement and injury outcomes in family and intimate assaults. *JAMA, 267*(22), 3043–3047.

16   Campbell, J.C., Webster, D., Koziol-McLain, J., Block, C., Campbell, D., Curry, M. A., Gary, F., Glass, N., McFarlane, J., Sachs, C., Sharps,

P., Ulrich, Y., Wilt, S., Manganello, J., Xu, X., Schollenberger, J., Frye, V., & Lauphon, K. (2003). Risk factors for femicide in abusive relationships: Results from a multisite case control study. *American Journal of Public Health, 93*(7), 1089–1097.

17   Violence Policy Center (2017). *When men murder women: An analysis of 2015 homicide data.* Retrieved from http://www.vpc.org/studies/wmmw2017

18   Smith, S. G.; Fowler, K. A., & Niolon, P. H. (2014). Intimate partner homicide and corollary victims in 16 states: National Violent Death Reporting System, 2003–2009. *American Journal of Public Health, 104*(3), 461–466. DOI: 10.2105/AJPH.2013.301582

19   Kivisto, A. J. & Porter, M. (2019). Firearm use increases risk of multiple victims in domestic violence homicides. *Journal of the American Academy of Psychiatry and the Law, 48*(1). DOI: 10.29158/JAAPL.003888-20

20   Amnesty International (2019). *Fragmented and unequal: A justice system that fails survivors of intimate partner violence in Louisiana, USA.* Retrieved from https://www.amnesty.org/download/Documents/AMR5111602019ENGLISH.PDF.

21   Violence Policy Center (2017). *When men murder women: An analysis of 2015 homicide data.* Retrieved from https://vpc.org/studies/wmmw2017.

22   Fridel, E. E. & Fox, J. A. (2019). Gender differences in patterns and trends in U.S. homicide, 1976-2017. *Violence and Gender, 6*(1), 27–36. doi: 10.1089/vio.2019.0005

23   Cooper, A. & Smith, E. L. (2011). *Homicide trends in the United States, 1980-2008.* Retrieved from http://www.bjs.gov/content/pub/pdf/htus8008.pdf.

24   Mize, K. D., & Shackelford, T. K. (2008). Intimate Partner Homicide Methods in Heterosexual, Gay, and Lesbian Relationships. *Violence and Victims, 23*(1), 98–114.

25   18 U.S.C. 922(g).

26   A protection order is qualifying for the purpose of triggering the federal firearms prohibition if it is a protection order that (1) is "is-

sued after a hearing of which such person [the respondent] received actual notice, and at which such person had an opportunity to participate"; and 2) restrains the respondent from threatening or violent conduct , makes findings of a credible threat to the petitioner or prohibits force likely to result in bodily injury. 18 U.S.C. 922(g)(8).

27 18 U.S.C. 925(a)(1).

28 18 U.S.C. 922(g)(9).

29 Ibid.

30 142 Cong. Rec. S11872-01.

31 *United States v. Hayes* (555 U.S. 415 (2009)).

32 18 U.S.C. 925(a)(1).

33 18 U.S.C. 921(a)(32).

34 18 U.S.C. 922(g)(8).

35 18 U.S.C. 921(a)(33).

36 *United States v. Hayes* (555 U.S. 415 (2009)); *United States v. Castleman* (134 S. Ct. 1405 (2014)); *Voisine v. United States* (136 S.Ct. 2272 (2016)).

37 18 U.S.C. 921(33)(B); 18 U.S.C. 922(g)(8).

38 18 U.S.C. 921(33)(B).

39 Zeoli, A. M., McCourt, A., Buggs, S., Frattaroli, S., Lilley, D., & Webster, D. W (2017). Analysis of the strength of legal firearms restrictions for perpetrators of domestic violence and their association with intimate partner homicide. *American Journal of Epidemiology*. doi: 10.1093/aje/kwx362

40 Ibid.

41 Ibid.

42 National Domestic Violence Hotline (2017). Unpublished.

43 Webster, D. W., Frattaroli, S., Vernick, J. S., O'Sullivan, C., Roehl, J., & Campbell, J. C. (2010). Women with protective orders report failure to remove firearms from their abusive partners: results from an exploratory study. *Journal of women's health (2002)*, 19(1), 93–98. https://doi.org/10.1089/jwh.2007.0530

DISSENT TO DISTRICT OF COLUMBIA V. HELLER

1   *Miller*, 307 U. S., at 178.

2   See *Lewis* v. *United States*, 445 U. S. 55, 65–66, n. 8 (1980).

3   see *Mitchell* v. *W. T. Grant Co.*, 416 U. S. 600, 636 (1974) (Stewart, J., dissenting)

4   The Nature of the Judicial Process 149 (1921).

5   1 Schwartz 266.

6   *Id.*, at 274.

7   *Id.*, at 324.

8   *Marbury* v. *Madison*, 1 Cranch 137, 174 (1803).

9   *Ante*, at 5.

10 *Ante*, at 4.

11 *Ante*, at 6.

12 *Ante*, at 63.

13 *Parker* v. *District of Columbia*, 478 F. 3d 370, 382 (CADC 2007).

14 *Ante*, at 19.

15 1 *Oxford English Dictionary* 634 (2d ed. 1989).

16 Brief for Professors of Linguistics and English as *Amici Curiae* 19.

17 1 S. Johnson, *A Dictionary of the English Language* (1755)

18 1 J. Trusler, *The Distinction Between Words Esteemed Synonymous in the English Language* 37 (1794).

19 *Ante*, at 15.

20 Act for Regulating and Disciplining the Militia, 1785 Va. Acts ch. 1, §3, p. 2

21 *Ante*, at 19.

22 *Ante*, at 63.

23 *Perpich* v. *Department of Defense*, 496 U. S. 334, 340 (1990).

24 3 J. Elliot, Debates in the Several State Conventions on the Adoption of the Federal Constitution 401 (2d ed. 1863) (hereinafter Elliot).

25 *Perpich*, 496 U. S., at 340.

26 Wiener, The Militia Clause of the Constitution, 54 Harv. L. Rev. 181, 182 (1940).

27 U. S. Const., Art. I, §8, cls. 12–16.

28 Art. II, §2.

29 Art. I, §8, cl. 16.

30 Elliot 379.

31 Elliot 659.

32 *Ibid.*

33 2 *Schwartz* 932–933; see The Complete Bill of Rights 182–183 (N. Cogan ed. 1997) (hereinafter Cogan).

34 2 Schwartz 912.

35 *Id.*, at 758, 761.

36 *Id.*, at 729, 735.

37 *Id.*, at 628, 662.

38 *Id.*, at 665.

39 Cogan 181.

40 2 Schwartz 674–675.

41 1 Papers of Thomas Jefferson 363 (J. Boyd ed. 1950).

42 Cogan 169.

43 *Ante*, at 17.

44 *Ante*, at 10.

45 307 U. S., at 178.

46 *Vasquez*, 474 U. S., at 266.

47 1 Stat. 271.

48 Ibid.

49 See *Perpich*, 496 U. S., at 341.

50 *Id.*, at 548.

51 *Id.*, at 553.

52 *Ante*, at 47 (quoting *Cruikshank*, 92 U. S., at 553)

53 See generally C. Lane, The Day Freedom Died: The Colfax Massacre, The Supreme Court, and the Betrayal of Reconstruction (2008).

54 *Id.*, at 264–265.

55 *Id.*, at 266.

56 *Perpich*, 496 U. S., at 341, and nn. 9–10.

57 Ch. 75, 44 Stat. 1059.

58 307 U. S., at 178.

59 *Ante*, at 49–51.

60 *Ante*, at 64.

HOW PEOPLE CAN TAKE ON THE NRA

1 Key Gun Violence Statistics, Brady Campaign to Prevent Gun Violence, http://www.bradycampaign.org/key-gun-violence-statistics (last accessed March 10, 2018).

2 Gun Violence by the Numbers, Everytown for Gun Safety, https://everytownresearch.org/gun-violence-by-the-numbers/ (last accessed March 10, 2018).

3 Gun Violence by the Numbers, Everytown for Gun Safety, https://everytownresearch.org/gun-violence-by-the-numbers/ (last accessed March 10, 2018).

4 Jamie Ducharme, "More Americans Than Ever Support Stricter Gun Laws, Poll Finds," *Time*, Feb. 20, 2018, http://time.com/5167216/americans-gun-control-support-poll-2018/.

5 Christopher Ingraham, "Nobody Knows How Many Members the NRA Has, But Its Tax Returns Offer Some Clues," *Wash. Post*, Feb. 26, 2018, https://www.washingtonpost.com/news/wonk/wp/2018/02/26/nobody-knows-how-many-members-the-nra-has-but-its-tax-returns-offer-some-clues/.

6 A Brief History of the NRA, National Rifle Association, https://home.nra.org/about-the-nra/.

7 Christopher Ingraham, "Nobody Knows How Man Members the NRA Has, But Its Tax Returns Offer Some Clues," *Wash. Post*, Feb. 26, 2018, https://www.washingtonpost.com/news/wonk/wp/2018/02/26/nobody-knows-how-many-members-the-nra-has-but-its-tax-returns-offer-some-clues/.

8 Hahrie Han, "Want Gun Control? Learn from the N.R.A.," *N.Y. Times*, Oct. 4, 2018, https://www.nytimes.com/2017/10/04/opinion/gun-control-nra-vegas.html.

9 Barbara Goldberg and Gina Cherelus, "Corporate Partners Cut Cord with NRA as Gun Control Debate Rages," Reuters, Feb. 23, 2018, https://www.reuters.com/article/us-usa-guns-boycott/corporate-partners-cut-cord-with-nra-as-gun-control-debate-rages-idUSKCN1G71OX.

10   NRA Firearm Training, National Rifle Association, https://
      firearmtraining.nra.org/

11   "How America's Gun Industry Is Tied To The NRA," NPR, March
      13, 2018, https://www.npr.org/2018/03/13/593255356/how-americas-
      gun-industry-is-tied-to-the-nra.

12   Edith Honan, "Poll Finds Gun Owners, Even NRA Members,
      Back Some Restrictions," https://www.reuters.com/article/us-usa-
      shooting-denver-guns/poll-finds-gun-owners-even-nra-members-
      back-some-restrictions-idUSBRE86O02O20120725.

13   Colleen L. Barry, Ph. D., et al, "After Newtown –Public Opinion
      on Gun Policy and Mental Illness," *New England Journal of
      Medicine*, March 21, 2013, http://www.nejm.org/doi/full/10.1056/
      NEJMp1300512?query=featured_home&.

14   Background Checks for Guns, National Rifle Association Institute
      for Legislative Action, Aug. 8, 2016, https://www.nraila.org/get-the-
      facts/background-checks-nics/.

15   Eric Lipton and Alexander Burns, "The True Source of the NRA's
      Clout: Mobilization, Not Donations," Feb. 24, 2018, https://www.
      nytimes.com/2018/02/24/us/politics/nra-gun-control-florida.html.

16   Chris McGreal, 'The NRA Didn't Tolerate Dissent Well:' How
      the Gun Lobby Stays on Message, *The Guardian*, Oct. 23, 2015,
      https://www.theguardian.com/us-news/2015/oct/23/national-rifle-
      association-gun-lobby-wayne-lapierre/

17   2015 IRS Form 990 for the National Rifle Association, https://
      projects.propublica.org/nonprofits/organizations/530116130.

18   Center for Responsive Politics, Outside Spending
      Summary 2016, National Rifle Association, https://
      www.opensecrets.org/outsidespending/detail.
      php?cycle=2016&cmte=National+Rifle+Assn (last accessed March
      14, 2018). https://www.opensecrets.org/outsidespending/contrib.
      php?cmte=C90013301&cycle=2016

19   Violence Policy Center, Blood Money II: How Gun Industry
      Dollars Fund the NRA, Sept. 13, 2015 http://www.vpc.org/studies/
      bloodmoney2.pdf.

20 Supporting the NRA, Midway USA, https://www.midwayusa.com/nra-support.

21 Walter Hickey, "Here's Who the NRA Really Represents," *Business Insider*, Dec. 19, 2012, http://www.businessinsider.com/the-nra-has-sold-out-to-the-gun-industry-to-become-their-top-crisis-pr-firm-2012-12.

22 Thank You for Purchasing a Firearm from Taurus, https://www.taurususa.com/pdf/NRA/Taurus-NRA-Free-Membership-Print.pdf.

23 Gun Rights vs. Gun Control, Center for Responsive Politics, https://www.opensecrets.org/news/issues/guns (last accessed March 13, 2018).

24 Id.

25 Common Cause analysis of numbers provided by the National Institute for Money in State Politics, https://www.followthemoney.org/show-me?f-fc=2&d-eid=1854#[{1|gro=y (last accessed March 14, 2018).

26 Gun Rights vs. Gun Control, Center for Responsive Politics, https://www.opensecrets.org/news/issues/guns (last accessed March 13, 2018).

27 Center for Responsive Politics, Outside Spending Summary 2016, National Rifle Association, https://www.opensecrets.org/outsidespending/detail.php?cycle=2016&cmte=National+Rifle+Assn (last accessed March 14, 2018).

28 Id.

29 Gun Rights vs. Gun Control, Center for Responsive Politics, https://www.opensecrets.org/news/issues/guns (last accessed March 13, 2018).

30 Center for Responsive Politics, Outside Spending Summary 2016, National Rifle Association, https://www.opensecrets.org/outsidespending/detail.php?cycle=2016&cmte=National+Rifle+Assn (last accessed March 14, 2018).

31 Peter Stone and Greg Gordon, "FBI Investigating Whether Russian

Money Went to the NRA to Help Trump," McClatchy, Jan. 23,
2018, http://www.mcclatchydc.com/news/nation-world/national/
article195231139.html.

32 Id.

33 Tim Mak, "Depth of Russian Politician's Cultivation of
NRA Ties Revealed," NPR, March 1, 2018, https://www.npr.
org/2018/03/01/590076949/depth-of-russian-politicians-cultivation-
of-nra-ties-revealed.

34 Protection of Lawful Commerce in Arms Act," National Rifle
Association Institute for Legislative Action," April 1, 2010, https://
www.nraila.org/articles/20100401/protection-of-lawful-commerce-
in-arms.

35 Mike McIntire, "Conservative Nonprofit Acts as a Stealth Business
Lobbyist," *New York Times*, April 21, 2012, http://www.nytimes.
com/2012/04/22/us/alec-a-tax-exempt-group-mixes-legislators-and-
lobbyists.html.

36 National Conference of State Legislatures, "Self Defense and 'Stand
Your Ground,'" March 9, 2017, http://www.ncsl.org/research/civil-
and-criminal-justice/self-defense-and-stand-your-ground.aspx/.

37 Adam Weinstein, "How the NRA and Its Allies Helped Spread a
Radical Gun Law Nationwide," June 7, 2012, *Mother Jones*, https://
www.motherjones.com/politics/2012/06/nra-alec-stand-your-
ground/.

38 Manuel Roig-Franzia, "Fla. Gun Law to Expand Leeway for
Self-Defense," April 25, 2005, *Washington Post*, http://www.
washingtonpost.com/wp-dyn/content/article/2005/04/25/
AR2005042501553.html.

39 John Nichols, "How ALEC Took Florida's 'License to Kill' Law
National, *The Nation*, March 22, 2012, https://www.thenation.com/
article/how-alec-took-floridas-license-kill-law-national/.

40 National Conference of State Legislatures, "Self Defense and 'Stand
Your Ground,'" March 9, 2017, http://www.ncsl.org/research/civil-
and-criminal-justice/self-defense-and-stand-your-ground.aspx/.

41   Lisa W. Foderaro and Kristin Hussey, "In Wake of Florida Massacre,
     Gun Control Advocates Look to Connecticut," *N.Y. Times*, Feb.
     17, 2018, https://www.nytimes.com/2018/02/17/nyregion/florida-
     shooting-parkland-gun-control-connecticut.html.

TIME TO BRING FEDERAL DOMESTIC VIOLENCE
GUN LAWS IN LINE WITH TODAY'S REALITY

1   Everytown for Gun Safety Support Fund's calculations using FBI
    Supplementary Homicide Reports, 2018 victims of firearm intimate
    partner homicide.

2   Everytown for Gun Safety Support Fund, *Ten Years of Mass Shootings in
    the United States*. New York: Everytown for Gun Safety Support Fund,
    2019, https://every.tw/1XVAmcc. Everytown defines a mass shooting as
    any incident in which four or more people are shot and killed, excluding
    the shooter.

3   April M. Zeoli and Jennifer K. Paruk, "Potential to Prevent Mass
    Shootings Through Domestic Violence Firearm Restrictions,"
    Criminology & Public Policy 19 (December 2019): 129-145.

4   Jacquelyn C. Campbell, Daniel Webster, Jane Koziol-McLain,
    Carolyn, Block, Doris Campbell, Mary Ann Curry, Faye Gary,
    Nancy Glass, Judith McFarlane, Carolyn Sachs, Phyllis Sharps,
    Yvonne Ulrich, Susan A. Wilt, Jennifer Manganello, Xiao Xu, Janet
    Schollenberger, Victoria Frye, and Kathryn Laughon, "Risk Factors
    for Femicide in Abusive Relationships: Results From a Multisite
    Case Control Study," *American Journal of Public Health* 93, no. 7 (July
    2003): 1089-1097.

5   Alexia Cooper and Erica L. Smith, *Homicide Trends in the
    United States, 1980-2008*. Washington, DC: US Department
    of Justice, November 2011. http://www.bjs.gov/index.
    cfm?ty=pbdetail&iid=2221; Everytown for Gun Safety analysis of
    FBI Supplementary Homicide Reports, 2000-2012.

6   Everytown for Gun Safety Support Fund, *Unchecked: Over 1
    Million Firearm Ads, No Background Checks Required*. New York:

Everytown for Gun Safety Support Fund, February 2019. https://
everytownresearch.org/unchecked/

7   Eleven states require only a point-of-sale check for sales by
unlicensed handgun sellers (CA, CO, DE, NM, NV, OR, PA, RI,
VA, VT, and WA); seven states require only a background check on
those sales pursuant to a purchase permit (HI, IA, IL, MA, MI, NE,
and NC); and four states (CT, MD, NJ, and NY) and Washington,
DC, require a background check on both occasions.

8   Judith M. MacFarlane, Jacquelyn C. Campbell, Susan Wilt, Carolyn
J. Sachs, Yvonne Ulrich, and Xiao Xu, "Stalking and Intimate
Partner Femicide," *Homicide Studies* 3, no. 4 (1999): 300-316.

9   T.K. Logan and Kellie R. Lynch, "Dangerous Liaisons: Examining
the Connection of Stalking and Gun Threats Among Partner Abuse
Victims," *Violence and Victims* 33, no. 3 (January 2018): 399-416.

10   April M. Zeoli, Alexander McCourt, Shani Buggs, Shannon
Frattaroli, David Lilley, and Daniel W. Webster, "Analysis of
the Strength of Legal Firearms Restrictions for Perpetrators of
Domestic Violence and Their Associations with Intimate Partner
Homicide," *American Journal of Epidemiology* 187, no. 11 (November
2018): 2365–2371.

11   Everytown for Gun Safety Support Fund's calculations using FBI
Supplementary Homicide Reports, 2018 victims of firearm intimate
partner homicide.

12   Zeoli et al., "Analysis of the Strength," 2365-2371.

13   "Reauthorize the Violence Against Women Act (H.R. 1585 /
S.2843)," Everytown for Gun Safety Fund, published January 2020.
https://every.tw/3ailOiA.

14   "Background Checks Save Lives and Protect Our Communities,"
Everytown for Gun Safety Fund, published January 8, 2019. https://
every.tw/2VmvHY8.

15   "Guns and Violence Against Women: America's Uniquely Lethal
Intimate Partner Violence Problem," Everytown for Gun Safety
Fund, published October 17, 2019. https://every.tw/2wYvfGm.

LOCAL LAWS AND LOCAL ENFORCEMENT ARE CRITICAL TO HALT GUN VIOLENCE BETWEEN INTIMATE PARTNERS

1   18 USC 921(a)(33)(A)(i).
2   Bureau of Alcohol, Tobacco and Firearms (2017). *Are local criminal ordinances "misdemeanors under State law" for purposes of 18 U.S.C. 922(d) (9) and (g)(9)?* Retrieved from https://www.atf.gov/firearms/qa/are-local-criminal-ordinances-misdemeanors-under-state-law-purposes-18-usc-922d9-and-g9.
3   U.S. v Pauler, N.16-3070 (10th Cir. 2017).

EXTREME RISK LAWS SAVE LIVES

1   Broward County case file reviewed by Giffords Law Center.
2   "Annual Gun Law Scorecard," Giffords Law Center, https://lawcenter.giffords.org/scorecard/.
3   Centers for Disease Control and Prevention, WISQARS Fatal Injury Data, https://www.cdc.gov/injury/wisqars/fatal.html.
4   James Silver, Andre Simons, and Sarah Craun, "A Study of the Pre-Attack Behaviors of Active Shooters in the United States between 2000 and 2013," U.S. Department of Justice Federal Bureau of Investigation, June 2018.
5   *Protecting the Next Generation: Strategies to Keep America's Kids Safe from Gun Violence*, Giffords Law Center, March 6, 2018, https://lawcenter.giffords.org/protecting-next-generation/.
6   "Santa Barbara shooter planned killing spree to exact revenge," CNN Wire, Mary 25, 2014, https://kdvr.com/news/nationalworld-news/report-deputies-nearly-caught-santa-barbara-shooter-before-his-rampage/.
7   American Foundation for Suicide Prevention, "Risk Factors and Warning Signs," https://afsp.org/aboutsuicide/risk-factors-and-warning-signs.
8   Centers for Disease Control and Prevention, Web-based Injury Statistics Query and Reporting System (WISQARS), "Fatal and

Non-fatal Injury Reports," last accessed Feb. 20, 2019, https://www. cdc.gov/injury/wisqars. Calculations based on 2013 to 2017.

9   *Confronting the Inevitability Myth: How Data-Driven Gun Policies Save Lives from Suicide,* Giffords Law Center, September 13, 2018, https:// lawcenter.giffords.org/report-on-gun-suicide-confronting-the-inevitability-myth/.

10   "Congresswoman Gabrielle Giffords Hails New Mexico Governor's Signing of Extreme Protection Order Bill into Law," Giffords, February 25, 2020, https://giffords.org/press-release/2020/02/new-mexico-extreme-risk-protection-order-signing/.

11   Jeffrey W. Swanson, et al., "Implementation and Effectiveness of Connecticut's Risk–based Gun Removal Law: Does it Prevent Suicides." *Law & Contemporary Problems* 80, (2017): 179–208; Jeffrey W. Swanson, et al., "Criminal Justice and Suicide Outcomes with Indiana's Risk-Based Gun Seizure Law." *The Journal of the American Academy of Psychiatry and the Law,* (2019).

12   Colleen L. Barry, et al., "Trends In Public Opinion On US Gun Laws: Majorities Of Gun Owners And Non–Gun Owners Support A Range Of Measures," *Health Affairs* 38, no. 10 (2019): 1727–1734.

13   "MEMO: How Local "Gun Sanctuaries" Threaten Public Safety," Giffords, January 17, 2020, https://giffords.org/press-release/2020/01/gun-sanctuaries-memo/.

14   Kelly Drane, Preventing the Next Parkland: A Case Study of the Use and Implementation of Florida's Extreme Risk Law in Broward County, Giffords Law Center, February 2020, http:// giffordslawcenter.org/broward.

15   Id.

16   Erin Donaghue, "Florida's 'Red Flag' Law, Passed After Parkland Shooting, is Thwarting 'Bad Acts,' Sheriff Says," CBS News, August 9, 2019, https://cbsn.ws/2C2I29J.

17   Greg Allen, "Florida Could Serve as Example for Lawmakers Considering Red Flag Laws," NPR, August 21, 2019, https://n.pr/2oDvAtT.

18   Id.